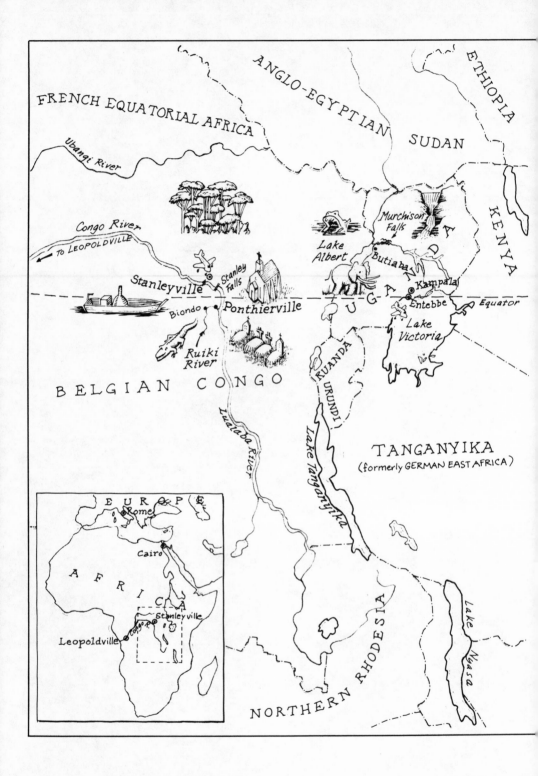

THE MAKING OF
The African Queen

THE MAKING OF

The African Queen

OR

How I Went to Africa with Bogart, Bacall and Huston and Almost Lost My Mind

KATHARINE HEPBURN

G.K.HALL &CO.
Boston, Massachusetts
1988

Published in Large Print by arrangement with
Alfred A. Knopf, Inc.

G.K. Hall Large Print Book Series.

Set in 18 pt Plantin.

Library of Congress Cataloging in Publication Data

Hepburn, Katharine, 1909–
    The making of the African Queen, or, How I went to Africa with
Bogart, Bacall and Huston and almost lost my mind / Katharine Hepburn.

    p. cm.—(G.K. Hall large print book series)
    "Published in large print"—T.p. verso.
    ISBN 0-8161-4650-0 (lg. print)
    1. African Queen (Motion picture) 2. Hepburn, Katharine, 1909–.
    3. Africa—Description and travel—1951-1976. 4. Motion picture
actors and actresses—United States—Biography. 5. Large type
books. I. Title II. Title: How I Went to Africa with Bogart,
Bacall, and Huston and almost lost my mind.
[PN1997.A31163H47   1988]
791.43'72—dc19   88–16470

To Mother and Dad

I've never written a diary—well, I mean, put down dreary things like when did my eye start twitching? when did it stop? why did it do it?—well, you know, things the doctor asks you and you've always forgotten them because they are really fundamentally dull.

Then, when you've lived as long as I have, you usually wish that you had kept one because you can't even remember the plot of many of the movies you've made—or the plays—really not anything about them or who or why.

But there are some happenings you can't forget. There they are. A series of facts—pictures—realities. This happened to me with *The African Queen*. I remember it in minute detail—I can see every second of its making and of me at the time of—

Well, I thought, so many people have asked me—What was it like? And I got to jotting down bits here—bits there—

And then I thought:

Come on, dear—pull it together.

So here it is—thirty-odd years after the fact.

THE MAKING OF
The African Queen

At a press conference—pretending to be adorable.

It was 1950—almost 1951. I was touring in *As You Like It* for the Theatre Guild. Trying to broaden my range and testing my talent.

"What are you going to do now?" Lawrence Langner (head of the Theatre Guild) had said immediately after the opening night of *The Philadelphia Story*.

"Good grief, Lawrence, what about this?"

"Yes. Fine. You've done it. What next?"

He's crazy, I thought.

A few years passed.

Well, if you don't improve you slip inevitably backward. Or you hammer—hammer—hammer on the same spot. And you become the same old thing doing the same old thing. He was right. Get going. So I had got going. I had persuaded Constance Collier to take me on as a pupil. I spent a thrilling time working with her on several of Shakespeare's plays.

Constance Collier was an English character actress living in New York and California. She had been brought up on Shakespeare. It was as much a part of her as fairy tales and Mother Goose were a part of my life. Rosalind—Viola—Juliet—Cleopatra—Beatrice—Katharina. She grew up with them as her constant companions. As I studied with Constance they became mine. It was exciting. I was so lucky to look upon these characters as real people—not people from another planet. It was fun too. She was a great teacher.

And here I was—Rosalind in *As You Like It*. It was lots of work but certainly I had broadened my horizon. And we were doing great business. We were in Los Angeles. I was living in Irene's house in Beverly Hills. Irene Selznick, that is. She's the daughter of Louis B. Mayer. She's my good friend. My dear friend. And I was lolling in the luxury of her beautiful big house. Tennis court. Swimming pool. Projection room— the screen rose up out of the floor as you pressed a button. The house faced south and was full of sunlight. There was Farr—the butler—who was an angel. Ida, his wife, very sweet to me. And a cook—Emily—who required much attention—at least half an hour of philosophical chat every day. But she could really cook, and as I love to eat, this was sheer heaven. Every meal—a treat—a total surprise. And not only to me, to anyone who came. And dessert—any dessert. You name it. Or it had no name. Thank you, Irene. Oh, thank you. Very very much.

Then the telephone rang. Well, that's what happens in our business. The telephone rings or a letter comes or flowers come with a card: May I call. This time it was the telephone.

"Hello, Miss Hepburn, I'm Sam Spiegel. I'm going to do a picture with John Huston —it's by C. S. Forester and it's called *The African Queen*. Have you read it?"

"No."

"Shall I send it to you? I'm anxious to know how you feel about it."

"Thank you. I'll read it right off."

Well, I read it. And it really made me sit up and take notice. Great part for me—Rosie—English—but that was O.K. I'd played a lot of English ladies. I called Sam.

"It's fascinating. Who's going to play what's his—yes—Charlie Alnutt?"

"I'll come to see you," said Spiegel.

He came and we talked about all the possible men—all English—because Charlie was supposed to have a cockney accent.

Then Sam said, "What about Bogart—he could be a Canadian."

"Why not?"

Now, looking back at that conversation —can you imagine anyone but Bogie playing that part? He was really it—hook, line and sinker.

As he was leaving, Spiegel turned to me:

"Do you know Bogart?"

"No," I answered.

"Do you know Huston?"

"No, Mr. Spiegel, I don't."

"He's really anxious to have you do it."

"That's very nice," I answered.

Spiegel started out the door, I stopped him.

"Where, Mr. Spiegel—Africa?"

"Well," he hesitated, "we'll see—"

"Oh no, sir," I said, "must be Africa—"

He smiled at me. "I'm so pleased that you like the book—"

"Yes, sir. So am I. But remember, it's Africa!"

Then I got a gorgeous bunch of flowers. Sam knows how to make you feel like something. Flowers. Champagne. "You are unique, Katie darling." Anyway, of course I said yes—I'm only human. Then they got Bogart.

Now—come on. Don't pretend. I know what you're wanting to know. Bogie. What was he like. What sort of a—You have to realize that I had no idea at all at this point what he was like. But I certainly found out. Making the picture and then afterward here and there. Now and then. And then even later, when he got sick—and then when he was very sick—then when he knew it was goodbye, Joe—and he was trying to make all of us feel O.K. about it. And he was too weak to walk up and down stairs. And he used to say, "Put me in the dumbwaiter and I'll ride down to the first floor in style. Come on—I'm a little guy—I'll fit."

Little guy? Did he say "little"? He was one of the biggest guys I ever met. He walked straight down the center of the road—

No maybes. Yes or no.

He liked to drink. He drank.

He liked to sail a boat. He sailed a boat.

He was an actor. He was happy and proud to be an actor.

He'd say to me, "Are you comfortable? Everything O.K.?"

He was looking out for me.

"Need anything?"

To put it simply: There was no bunk about Bogie. He was a man.

And on that last day, when Spence patted him on the shoulder and said, "Good-night,

Bogie," Bogie turned his eyes to Spence very quietly and with a sweet smile covered Spence's hand with his own and said—"Goodbye, Spence."

Spence's heart stood still. He understood.

Bogie meant it. He was on his way.

Goodbye, Spence.

Oh, dear. Well, don't get me going about Bogie. Come on—back to the beginning.

John Huston came to call. Have you ever met him? He came—came with Spiegel. I'd never met him. He's pretty—well, unique.

Then he came again.

Then he came again.

Watch it. Watch it, Katie. It's a good story—but remember what happened with that other charmer! I don't get his message —that's all. Well, so what—he's right up there. Could it be pure snobbery that makes me want to do the thing at all? *Treasure of the Sierra Madre* was great and Walter (John's father) was sensational. Oh, I don't know. How much of it does he write himself? I don't even know that he's read the book, for he sure seems to be stumbling around. And why does he always come protected? I've never even seen him without Sam or Bogart or some *big man*. A newspaper man usually. Anyway, heaven knows what they were talking about. And then the rush for drinks. And then out. Oh—and later . . .

Answer me one thing. Why can't he be on time? I'm working a million times harder than he is. Eight performances of *As You Like It* every week. Oh, forget it. I think it will be a perfectly ghastly experience and I'm sure the script will stink and I certainly don't know why I'm doing it at all.

And those stories. And that studied old-Kentucky-colonel charm. Frankly, at Irene's at lunch one day, he started about some Mexican character and I couldn't keep my mind on what he was talking about, he proceeded so slowly. Well . . . maybe he's great. I don't know. But he makes me uneasy. I feel all hands and feet and I simply can't imagine being directed by him. Frankly, I think he's one of the over-masculine boys who fascinate themselves and the New York critics being great guys, and, oh well, I hope I'm wrong.

"Katie dear."

"What?"

"Sam says you're worried about the script—"

"Well—"

"Don't you worry, honey—"

"Maybe you'd prefer it if I never mentioned the script."

"Oh no, my dear, I want to know what you think—"

But somehow none of this rang true and certainly nothing materialized. And so I wound up just forcing it out of my mind. I did want to go to Africa and I felt it would be my only chance. So what the hell. Maybe John just wanted to go to Africa too.

We went on to San Francisco with *As You Like It*, after an utterly unsatisfactory three weeks in Los Angeles during which time I felt that Huston was deliberately avoiding me. And I must say, my impressions of him were a total blank. Couldn't make hide nor hair of him. What he thought of the script —what he was going to do—where they were going to do it. I'd talked to Walter Strohm of Metro, who had made all the arrangements out there for *King Solomon's Mines*. He said there were no good rivers in Kenya. I told Huston and just got, "Well, now, that's very interesting, dear. Is that so?" He made me feel a kind of nuisance and dumbbell. Was I?

Time passed. *As You Like It* ended. *The African Queen*'s starting date was coming up. Vagueness continued. No script appeared.

Huston went to London. Reports came back that he was very ill with flu. This I didn't believe but my inclination . . . Oh, I did forget to tell you that I saw his *Asphalt Jungle* and felt it to be a bit sloppy from the script angle. Told him so in an effort to jolt him. He just smiled and said, "Is that so, dear. Interesting." He put one constantly on the defensive, as I was always in the position of exposing my point of view and getting a perfectly blank reaction. Anyhow, I did not believe for an instant that he was ill. Just thought he was fascinating around and not working.

After endless on-again-off-again wires concerning the business aspects, here I was sitting in New York waiting frantically for ACTION. Constance Collier and her secretary, Phyllis Wilbourn (who is now my secretary and companion), were to travel with me to London. We had no idea whether there was enough money to make the picture. There was no new script. Spiegel had slipped me an early one which I thought left a lot to be desired. There were romantic declarations as to the need for my immediate arrival. There were warm telegrams of condolence on the sudden death of my mother (later it turned out that he didn't know that she was dead or

9

didn't remember). Now, did he even know that these wires had been sent? I haven't the least idea—I don't even think he has any idea. Or perhaps he has. I wonder.

Finally, I thought it would be a good idea to just go—and my agents thought it was all more or less set. Mind you, I believe I was doing what I wanted to. I wanted to go. — At least I think I did. Hard to find a good story. But was this a good story? Where am I?

So in a state of total fury, insecurity and indecision, we departed on a small boat—the *Medea*. Due to arrive in Liverpool eight days later. It was early April. Understanding the apathy of big-city newspapers to get interviews with movie stars unless they had just committed arson, murder or rape, I arrived deliberately just too far away for them to bother. And the local press, always less persistent, contented themselves with photographs. Carefully attired in my leather coat and tan suit with a handkerchief around my neck to cover my most evident area of decay, I got off the boat. Immigration had come to our cabin—delightful consideration—and we had only to locate our various baggage. We were met by a station wagon and a huge

Rolls-Royce and a publicity lady named Miss Dipper.

We set off for London. An eight-hour trip. As usual, if there's no bathroom available—I need to go to the bathroom. Also I wanted to telephone my old friend in England to avoid the terror of arriving in a place and then realizing that I had arrived and that no one could care less. I asked Miss Dipper whether we could find a bathroom in a gas station. No . . . they only had them in hotels and we couldn't very well go in without also staying for breakfast. Could we? Since we'd just had it five times waiting for the boat to land, I had to agree with her. Finally we found a telephone booth on the side of the road. I called my London number and had a lengthy discussion with the operator, only to decipher that she was trying to tell me that the number had been disconnected: "ceased line," she called it. As Miss Dipper then had several calls to make, I had an opportunity to scrutinize the landscape for a possible bathroom. Across the highway was a stone wall and there seemed to be a sort of park on the other side. In desperation I scaled the wall.

Oh—let me not forget to tell you. There was a message given to me that everything was set. This from Sam Spiegel. Said Miss

Dipper, "I was told to tell you that everything is set and here is a letter from Mr.
Huston." I opened it. I was informed that
it was perfectly lovely that I was in England
and that the one person to do the clothes was
a woman (whose name I can't remember)
who was a really remarkable designer. And
then there were several rough pen sketches
by Mr. Huston himself. You must just take
my word for it that the letter did not quite
make sense. Nor the sketches. Especially as
I had not read his script, nor had I talked to
him for four months, nor had we ever dis-
cussed clothes. And why send the letter all
the way to Liverpool? My only reaction was
that he must be living with whoever it was
and that she had said, What about the letter, and that he had sat down to write it on
the spur of the moment. Later in our ac-
quaintance, he sat down on the spur of the
moment to write one of these for the black
boy who was taking care of him and I said,
Don't overdo it.

So with April snow falling on the Midland
Hills, we arrived finally, eight hours later,
in London. Went to Claridge's. The room
was literally full of flowers—mostly for Constance. But quite a few for me too. I had
been informed that there was to be a large

press conference on Monday—this was Saturday— but that the leading-light columnists would like to see me before the conference.

I couldn't see the sense of a general press conference if I loused up all the rest of the people at the conference by giving these two men a twenty-four-hour lead. So I said no.

We got unpacked and Huston—Spiegel —and the brothers John and Jimmy Woolf, our English producers, came to call. How do you do and all the folderol. I did find out that John really had been quite ill. One speck of truth. Of course, no script to either Spiegel or the Woolf brothers. Just John and John and John and John. Because when Huston is present everyone focuses attention on him, exactly as when there is a small child in the room.

I'd already found out through my friend Michael Benthall—the man who directed *As You Like It*—that *his* choice for advice on the clothes would be Doris Langley Moore, who had a Museum of Costume. The clothes must look real and not like a fancy-dress party. They—my friends Bobby Helpmann and Michael Benthall—knew about the woman Huston had mentioned and said that she would be no good at all. Having dinner with Bobby and Michael my first night, I had immediately inquired about this, because I knew that Huston must really want this woman or he never would have written that note.

Next day, Sunday, I was in bed with the curse and a terror of the press conference and a general horror at being in London at all. Huston called to say that a man named Gourlay—a reporter—was in his room and would I come down. He was one of the two columnists. I said no and stated my point about not undermining the conference. Privately I thought, Well, I'm sure they're probably both down there drinking and the price of the liquor is right on the picture. He urged a bit—very shrewdly. I didn't take the bait. Then he agreed with the nobility of my stand and my great fairness of character and we planned to have a drink with Mr. Gourlay after the big conference. Later, John appeared in my room and tried to urge me, but again very quickly abandoned it. Yes, we would have a drink after the general conference. One day . . .

The conference—terrifying—but went pretty well. Stood for two and one half hours. Drinking milk. Shouldn't let them get my goat so. Bogarts—Betty and Bogie— were there, and Huston and Sam Spiegel, of course. Finally it ended. Gourlay—the sour journalist—didn't come and afterward broke a drink date with Huston and me just to be able to write something disagreeable about me being the poor man's Garbo. That I'd refused to see him. A lie. Dear—dear—and what am I supposed to do, and who cares?

So: launched in London and through with the press. All the interviews started with "forty-one-year-old K.H." Or "thin" . . . or "freckled." And when Judy Garland came, it was "twenty-seven-year-old"—"fat" —"double-chinned." Wonderful story how she found a reporter sitting on the floor below her with camera poised and she said very politely, "What do you want?" And he said, "I'm waiting to get a picture of your double chin." I adore the press!

Anyway: Now to get down to true bones on the picture. I told you that I had had an early script which Sam Spiegel had slipped me. I'd read it again on the boat. The first part very generally speaking seemed O.K. But from the love scene on it seemed to sag. The getting into the love scene seemed too abrupt and—well, no use going into details. But I thought that there would be serious trouble with a lot of it.

It was now Tuesday—April 17th—Huston

had made no effort to see me or talk about the script. On costumes we'd had one talk. I told him that I didn't want his woman; I wanted Langley Moore and I would go to see what she had in the museum. Also, she'd been born in Africa and knew of missionaries from a grandparent who was one. He said fine. He gave up so easily on his choice, I was taken aback. His lady was never mentioned again.

Next day I saw Langley Moore. She had a really great collection, even down to Victoria's underpants with a fifty-inch waistline—fascinating stuff. I'd borrow things from her to take back to the hotel to show to Huston. He was working with Peter Viertel on the script and I was the only one to have time to do anything else. Handle him with care. Keep him working. When I got one of the costumes on I'd call downstairs and he and Peter would come up. I had underclothes too. All the most hideous things he adored. And the grotesque underwear. He wanted to visit the museum. We went. Mrs. Langley Moore showed us all sorts of clothes. He made me put on a combination and said that that was what I would play most of the picture in. A combination, incidentally, was a one-piece sort of shirt and pants combined. It is either split fore and aft for facility in the bathroom or it had a tab between the legs to hold it down. It was mid-thigh—this one was split fore and aft. My heart sank. I wondered just how stubborn he would turn out to be. He was fascinated by the clothes, the jewelry, the trunks, and it wasn't five minutes before Doris Langley Moore had sensed what it is that apparently everyone senses—that Huston was the center of the stage. Everything swings around him and his moods. Would he come? Would he keep concentrating? Others were expected to be the solid rock on which he built.

I wandered around in the combination feeling a perfect ass and showing mine. And wondering exactly how poor Jack Cardiff was going to be able to photograph me (a lady of uncertain age) in such a garment.

Yes—oh yes, dear—very interesting—oh, excellent—that's very good. In a sort of dream and with little discussion and a vague series of "Well"s and "Isn't that grand"s—suddenly we had chosen the wardrobe and I was back at the hotel. I had the curious feeling that he hadn't seen *me* in the clothes at all. Then Bogart's clothes were chosen. Something about a blue shirt with a place to fasten a collar button. His clothes were actually ordered. I had no idea whether or not I was to go ahead with mine but at least I knew what they were to be in a dream sort of way.

The script. I couldn't just let this ride. I must take a stand, or a hand, or something. I called him and immediately he said, "Come on down, dear—I was going to call you." I went down. "What about the love scene?" "Well, now, Peter and I were just talking. Just what is your notion about that? Say what you said the other day."

I'd hardly got into the room—sat down —found a cigarette. . . . All my thoughts had been collected to bring him back from some idiotic topic to the script and here he was talking about it and asking me to. Here's my chance. I'd better be impressive.

He listened (he always does) and oh, my friend, let me warn you, he remembers everything. Absolutely everything. Only twice—when he was drunk or more or less so and intentionally more or less so—have I known him to forget anything. Well, then he goes the other way, for he doesn't re-member anything.

So I launched forth about love and pas-sion. I thought that I was pretty good. I sug-gested the bit about the kiss being after the success of the rapids—and the throwing the hat away—the symbol of propriety. In the book she kissed his foot when he hurt it. I couldn't imagine a straitlaced lady kissing a foot. And the thought of me kissing Bogart's foot was just funny. But . . .

"Honey, what will you have to drink? Say, have you ever done any hunting?"

"Well, no—nothing. And no, I haven't. But if they kiss before . . ." And a bold attempt to reattract, but we were off to the races. I was shown his riding boots, all of them. His pink coat—his britches—his vests—his socks—his silk hat—in fact, he put them on. The silk hat suited him. His funny little face and scrawny neck took on a country-squire look. His fascination with each article and whether I had ever ridden to hounds was evident. His eyes lit up. Well, we were about as far from the *Queen* as we could get and Mr. H. seemed delighted. So, there we were. The script was pages too long. I thought very poor in places. I couldn't actually get after the clothes or test or proceed in any direction because of financial matters (unsettled). Huston was leaving for Africa in forty-eight hours—and I was frothing at the mouth with disgust at the whole lackadaisical atmosphere. Save your breath

19

to blow your porridge, Kathy. You might as well give up.

Drinks were being poured—the telephone was ringing. Frankly, I didn't see any way that the picture could ever possibly be made. And I felt exactly as though I were conducting the last desperate moments of an extremely unsatisfactory love affair with Mr. Huston. Verging on the actively unpleasant.

I called him the next day. He was out. Never called me back. In frustrated disgust, I drove to Manchester with Michael Benthall. It was a relief. When I got back he had gone to Africa, leaving everything and especially me shattered. Actually, everyone else seemed to think the script was great, and I never said what I thought to anyone except Constance. There was the most awful turmoil about dollars and sterling and this and that. I ordered the clothes, feeling that they would never be used and thinking that I might have to pay for them myself.

Bogie and I met for a serious chat. You may have gathered by this time that I was a bit of a busybody and worrier. This sort of vagueness about everything—scripts, money and so forth—really bothered me.

"What are we going to do?" I said to Bogie.

"Well," he said, "we're here—we liked it—we'll do it. Working with John is always a bit—well—you know—like this."

"You mean—just shut up and do it—?"

"Yes—why not—they'll find the money. They have to—"

"I hope you're right," I said.

"I'm right," he said. His was a simple approach: All the elements were there—it will work—don't fuss.

I finally said to Christopher Mann (my agent) that no matter what—pay or no pay —I was going to do the picture. And I didn't want to talk about it anymore.

My main object then being to get to Africa, where I could again try to see whether I could have any influence on the script. It was at this point that I asked Dad to send me a letter of credit for ten thousand dollars so that I could move out fast if I had to.

John and Peter Viertel were in Africa. Supposedly they were cutting the script and fixing up certain scenes—picking locations, etc. We were to leave the 13th of May to join them. By dint of the brilliant speed of various English shoemakers, boots were made in four days by Dolcis, who had a Polish cavalry officer who knew how to make ladies' button boots. The people at Victor

21

Stiebel's made the clothes and underclothes and hats. All organized by Doris Langley Moore. And Bogart's one costume was made at Berman's.

I stumbled onto the airplane for Rome. Constance and Phyllis remained in London. The *African Queen* Company were to leave from Rome. Betty and Bogie were there already. Spence was on his way from New York to Naples by boat. I was to stay with my friend Fran Rich, who was studying sculpture in Rome and had an apartment there. She came to the Ciampino Airport to pick me up in her little Fiat Giardinetta station wagon. No paparazzi! What luck! We drove into the city by the old Appian Way—it is now closed to public transport. Two thousand years of history. It was started in 312 B.C. as a military highway from Rome. It was fascinating. We dumped my junk at her apartment and then drove all over Rome by the light of the moon.

Next day we took a picnic to Ostia Antica, which was the old port of Rome at the mouth of the Tiber River. It had been silted in with muck and sand erosion and more or less completely abandoned as early as 827 A.D. Then it was excavated, beginning in 1854. We visited the ruins—the theatre—the

Neptune Baths—we picked wild flowers. An experience.

The following day we drove to Naples to pick up Spencer. "What's that?" he said, looking at our little Fiat. Needless to say, we switched cars with the M-G-M limousine sent to pick him up. Someone else drove our little one back to the city. Spence stayed at the Grand Hotel. Fran would get him and deliver him. We had a glorious time—picnics, sightseeing, churches, dinners in Fran's flat with the local friends, walks in the country. Spencer loved Rome. The press never caught on that I was in Rome too. We drove all over the place, but they never got a picture of us together or of any kind, except at the end, when Fran took me to the plane for Africa. Then we posed for them—Fran and I posed, I mean, not Spencer. No. Spencer had left the day before for London. Did he leave because he was bored or did he leave because he couldn't bear to say goodbye? The eternal question.

So off I went.

There were eight berths on the plane—you could lie down on planes in those days. The Bogarts had the lower and I had the upper above them. There were about twenty members of our troupe; the rest were strangers. The strangers had the other berths between us and the ladies' room.

I have never had any idea what goes on with other people—but I have found that my major concern in traveling in foreign parts is where is the ladies' room. Now, in an airplane it always seems that it is as far away from me as possible. And that the more complicated and embarrassing the trip, the more frequent my desire to make it. This is bad enough for an ordinary citizen. But if you are a so-called well-known public personality, it is awful to have the excitement of your kidneys common knowledge. Any excitement makes mine weak. Hell—even in my adolescent days of football games at the Yale Bowl I was in such an agony in this respect that I determined early to pick a trade which would keep me away from the Yale Bowl. It wasn't worth it. It was thus that I became an actor. A simple and practical reason.

Anyhow, time came to go to bed. The berths were let down. I thought of my early-morning trip down the length of the plane and wished that I'd decided not to make the picture. Imagine my joy when I got into my berth and discovered that they had provided what looked like a cardboard pot. The electric light in my berth was on the blink but I had a searchlight. Read for a while. Slept. Four o'clock the urge. The pot. The joy of privacy. Oh no! To my horror—my deep horror—oh God—my horror—my foot—damp—the pot—my God—it wasn't—but what—a hole in the bottom—oh no—the bed—the sheets—the bed, it was wet—just plain wet—I had deliberately wet the bed—oh no—the Bogarts—what—reached? No—the mattress—oh—sponge rubber—and the sheets—a complete envelope case—next morning when the steward makes it up—no—don't think—sleep, don't think.

So I traveled to Africa. In the morning they just folded it all back into the plane. I laughed and laughed and cried all by myself. But why do I spend my life in such ways? I hope this bathroom talk doesn't offend you. Please just remember that I'm the daughter of a urologist—hell, I'm the sister of a urologist too.

Léopoldville, practically on the Equator, was our first destination. Heat—damp—a barrage of amateur photographers—long flat-field-flat-town—very kind people. Heat—hotel—French-speaking Belgians—no panes of glass in windows—porches—high ceilings—blinds—mosquito nets over beds—

As you see, I arrive in Africa with Betty and Bogie.

painted cement floors—dark, spare bathroom—watch the bugs—watch the water—thoughtful people—took care of us afternoon and evening. We went to bed early. Up at 4:00 a.m. And off again.

Stanleyville. Belgian Congo. Peter Viertel met us. One hour before, John Huston had taken off for our village at Biondo. Did you hear what I said? *One* hour before. We had flown halfway around the world to get to him. And one hour before, he had left on a private plane for our camp, which was just being completed—south—down the Congo River about eight hours by rail and then west into the jungle by car another forty miles and no telephone. I can't describe my emotions. You see, I didn't know any of these people. The Bogarts seemed sweet but I didn't know them. Peter Viertel? Well, I knew his mother, Salka Viertel, and he seemed nice. But, gosh, I couldn't be entirely honest with him. Not only had Huston gone to Biondo but he had taken his guns with him. Not the script! To this day he has never told me why he left. I suppose he was absolutely horrified at the thought of beginning the picture, and the sight of us was the knell of doom. It was an utterly piggish thing to do and it makes me mad to think of it even now—goddamn—goddamn. . . .

If Peter Viertel, the writer, had not met us, no one would have. Dear Peter Viertel. He saved my sanity—he sort of took me over and filled my time with golf and trips here and there and talk about the script. Peter Viertel was an absolute angel to me— to everyone. Helpful—kind—and a damned good writer. He eventually wrote a fascinating book about two men, *White Hunter, Black*

Heart, sort of inspired by this experience. Thank God he was there.

Stanleyville is quite a charming town. Also hot. Also humid. But a bit more pep in the air than Léo. It is also on the Congo River. And pretty flat too.

We were taken to our hotel, the Pourquoi Pas. Right on the Congo. Lovely view. Consisting of two parts—the eating and drinking building, and the sleeping building. The latter three-storied. It had an outside staircase. I had been put into a room on the ground floor on the street—a dark, dismal room where everyone could look in the window. The Bogarts were up on the top floor with a lovely porch looking down the river.

I nearly fainted with rage and frustration. Who the hell had arranged the rooms! Wasn't I as good as Bogie! I went to the manager. No reaction. Then I asked who else in the company was housed there. I found out that the accountant and auditor, who had been there for some time, had a lovely room next to the Bogarts. Without a wasted step, without a thought of them or their rights of possession, and certainly with not a word to either of them—I walked into their room . . . threw everything into suitcases and demoted them to my room on the first floor. Then I cleaned up the mess, assisted by Peter Viertel, and unpacked my junk. I felt guilty but not quite guilty enough not to dispossess them.

We were to stay in Stanleyville killing time, as far as I could see, until we were sent to Biondo. Frustrated rage was my constant mood. Messages came through from the camp at Biondo that Mr. H. would like an elephant permit for the Belgian Congo. He had already done some hunting in Uganda while looking for locations and he would like to do more in the Congo. The license cost three hundred dollars. This, I supposed, would go down as an expense necessary to the picture. My rage increased. Supposedly we were getting appropriate clothes, etc., for the jungle. Nothing arrived for me but I couldn't have cared less, as my own wardrobe was much more suitable to the jungle than it has ever been anywhere else. I may look odd walking across Claridge's lobby but I'm the height of chic in the jungle.

I wish I could describe Stanleyville to you. The Congo River stretches along—lots of curves—just about as wide as the Connecticut River. Banks flattish on either side. Villages—palm trees—jungle scrub. Unfortunately, just south of Stanleyville are rapids.

The same is true at Léopoldville and just above Ponthierville too. Thus the river is not navigable. One must occasionally transfer to the train—in 1951, a Toonerville Trolley—then back to the river. They want to cut canals, but this is expensive.

There's a lot of river life. Sidewheelers. Barges. Tugs. And pirogues. The latter a native canoe cut out of a single tree and hollowed out. They might be full of bananas—wood—bricks—the family—the nursing baby. They felt most unsteady, but let's face it, so do ours. They have paddles according to the size of the canoes. And carved according to the capacity of the owner. I've seen canoes so deep that, standing up, I could hardly see over the edges. Or too small for Bogie's bottom. They weigh a ton and they are not painted. It's fascinating in a sullen, gusty thunderstorm to see them all make for shore. They have storms down there. The river gets choppy and the palm trees blow and the sky gets black as pitch, and yellow. It rains like mad and everyone gets soaked. Especially the mud roads. You dry off fast but the roads don't. The mud roads are a great problem, because five minutes after a rain starts the roads become impossible and impassable. Thank heaven for

Abercrombie and Fitch and lightweight rubber overshoes. My clothes were incredible. I found that out. And luckily I had something for every occasion. And everything was washable. White. My Mexican hat most appropriate.

People are afraid of the African sun— but oddly it didn't seem to bother me, at least while playing golf. Otherwise I wore my straw Mexican sombrero. Many people say dark glasses are more important than the sun helmet. Who knows? Everyone does something different. I had a kind of stuff to protect my skin from the glare, being very freckled—and it worked. Aided by long sleeves and high necks.

Did I tell you about the water? Well, have you ever been to Atlanta, Georgia? There the water is soft. Like velvet. Well, here it's like honey. It is the most spectacular water. Dirt evaporates. You may have to pick spiders out of the tub, or ants. And flying objects attracted by the electric lights or a lizard may drop on you from above. And the inside of the tub may be peeling off. And the shower head, if there is one, may have very few openings. But what does any of this matter if the water is soft and cleanses rather than dries? Fantastic. You can have the most elaborate suite with the finest plumbing—but to what end if the fundamental liquid—the soul of the bathroom—the inhabitant of the pipe, the shower, the tub, the washbasin without the water—is, as it is in most cities—London, Paris, Rome, Chicago—a drying liquid guaranteed to remove skin if it removes dirt and to turn hair into straw. Here it is sheer heaven and no need at all for any lubricant.

Of course you can't drink it. It's poison. In fact, they say you shouldn't even brush your teeth in it. But, my oh my, the feeling! Luscious. Angel's fingers stroking you.

My bedroom is quite charming. I sleep under a net. Hard bed. Straw pillow. Two french windows. A balcony over the Congo. And cement floors again painted red—they come off on the soles of your shoes and feet. A wardrobe—a desk—a table—two comfortable chairs. I can see the sunset—the river life. I can hear the drums at night in the native village across the river. My clothes are always damp. And the towels smell like baby's diapers and the cigarettes are hard to draw and soft. The glue on the envelopes sticks—empty ones, I mean. Your stamps don't—except together. Your shoes and leather baggage are in no time covered with mold. Scissors rust. It's damp.

Motion is slow—especially between 10:00 a.m. and 4:00 p.m. Most activity of an athletic nature takes place before 10:00 or after 4:00.

It takes quite a while to arrange anything. The difficulty of the language. The blacks speak varieties of Swahili and broken French. The Belgians, French. They had a hell of a time understanding me. Breakfast on a tray served in my room was something which I never could explain. I am a very early riser, and I used to get up—bathe—dress—go down three outside flights of stairs. Past the houseboys—two on each landing. *"Jambo"* (good morning, hello), *"jambo."*

Into the building. Through the bar still covered with the sins of the night before and into the dining room. There I would order sliced pineapple. Simply great. *Oeufs sur plat* —toast—coffee. Put it on a tray and carry it back to my room. It took anywhere from fifteen minutes to one hour to get the breakfast. I could not figure out why the difference. But not to worry, for it did no good at all. Sometimes it—the breakfast—was hot. Sometimes cold. Then back up the stairs with the tray. The houseboys still sitting on

33

their stair landings in the sun, polishing shoes. They found my trip back up the stairs with the tray hilarious. My quick pace ludicrous. In fact, life itself they approach with a great sense of humor and a broad smile. They wear a round white stitched cap. And white sort of loose gowns to the knees, buttoning high to the neck—like the ones the Russians wear. And a wide tight stitched belt—usually red—and bare feet. They say yes to everything and then they do what they usually do. With a prayer that they have guessed you aright. It is rather fascinating, and full of lovely surprises. And you realize what an enormous barrier it is not to understand either the language or the habits. And you begin to learn patience. They have learned it—you see. It used to take us two hours to order and eat lunch. Three hours for dinner. If we ordered different things it made no matter, we'd get the same. And served at the time that they expected us to eat.

The locals were charming to us and gave us lifts in their cars. Invited us to play golf at their club. A nice little nine-hole course, very flat but with many trees. It was cut out of the jungle, and huge anthills, forty or fifty feet high like great cornucopias upside down, are the hazards. Nice greens, and the rough always being kept down by blacks whisking with pieces of metal about two inches wide and four feet long and sharp on each side. The caddies are tiny black boys. One carries the bag. Another the extra balls. Another watches the ball and another, any personal possessions. They are wildly anxious for the job. Each time we played we had to fight them off—fifty strong—all the way through the clubhouse to the first tee, and then twenty-five would play the first hole with us. Finally after much shooing away and waving of golf clubs, they would depart. They were out to join us again on the ninth green. So we always paid on the ninth tee to avoid confusion.

There are excellent shops and fascinating printed cottons worn by the black ladies. These are made in Belgium and in England and sent out for the local trade. Some are geometric. Most are covered with snails, shells, starfish. Some with the King and Queen of England or the King and Queen of Belgium. All in wonderful colors or black and white. The ladies make a low-cut blouse. Then they wind on yard goods to make a skirt or a turban or both. Often a baby is slung on the back in part of the

35

drapery. It is fascinating to see a glorious portrait pulled tight across the generous bottom of a local lady moving along the street. There goes the Prince of Wales.

I bought an aluminum steamer trunk. Two white shirts. Bolts of yard goods. Two petrol stoves. (There had to be petrol available for their generators.) Two thermos bottles. Three stewing pots. A double boiler. Looking ahead, I was: hot water for hair washing or hot soup or . . . The shops were like our general stores.

Killing time—killing time. Hired a pirogue and was rowed across the Congo with Peter Viertel to visit a fishing village. They sling nets shaped like huge icecream cones —made of bamboo and hemp braced with stakes—into the rapids. The fisherfolk look healthier than the rest who look rickety. Thin legs and the calf anywhere from ankle to knee. Poorly. But straight backs and square shoulders. Women too. Or women especially, for they carry the most alarming objects on their backs and heads—anything from a can of peaches to a cord of wood to a bunch of bananas to a pail of water. The women do all the heavy work. They wear a kind of round cushion four inches in diameter on their heads to make balancing easier.

They part their hair front to back in about five or six horizontal lines, one and a half inches apart. Then they braid what's left between the tracks. Being quite short and curly, the braid lies very flat for it's made of short strands picked up and worked along. A nice design, quite fascinating, and a style quite common here now.

Hunting vaguely for interesting objects, we bought spears and carved oars and all manner of carved stools. And a wonderful chair. They were sweetly carved in simple, childish geometric designs. No figures. You made an offer and usually they would part with it. Then others would come running out with more. The little village was made of mud huts constructed on bamboo frames with thatched palm roofs. They cook outside on wood and in a sort of crock jar. In the Congo, they eat rice as a base, and bananas and pineapple. In Uganda, maize is the base. Their stomachs protrude. You don't see many old ones—venereal disease, malaria and sleeping sickness do them in. They like to dance to the beat of drums made of hollowed-out logs. Small drums two feet long —big drums ten feet long, maybe two feet in diameter, or even more. And a strange small wood box-like instrument with metal strips—

eight or ten strips fastened down, which they flick with their thumbs. Very primitive and repetitive. And they chant. Odd, but I had the impression that we put them off. They were reluctant to sort of show off to us— they didn't really trust us. Who can blame them. Usually someone understood French and they would help us bargain. They loved a joke.

Next day we told Betty and Bogie about the fishing village and they wanted to see it. We went to hire a motorboat, this time to cross the river. The motorboats are often metal. The one we found had been standing all day with the engine cover on. It was very hot. The black man who ran it came onto the boat in a hurry—cast off, for he knew that we'd been waiting for him. He threw back the cover. Spun the wheel to start the engine. There was a terrific explosion. Petrol in the bilge. It was full of fumes from the heat and being covered. The spark ignited it.

Bogie, who had been leaning over the engine, luckily stood up just before the ignition was turned on. Otherwise he would have got the blast full in the face.

The flames were twenty feet high. The black man had got hit on the inside of his arms and thighs. Skin hanging—a frightful sight. He started to rip off his shorts. Remembered that ladies were there. Grabbed a pail. Dived overboard, we thought gone for good. But back he came with a bucket of sand to save his boat, He must have been in agony. People on the dock just stood like idiots. We tried to throw the rope to people standing on the shore. We were drifting out. We went past another boat and they caught the rope. Bogie leaped across and grabbed their fire extinguisher and tried it on the flames. No effect. The flames were quieting down but were still very hot in the engine box. I had visions of us going up like a fire-cracker. I am a complete coward where fire is concerned. Bogie, completely courageous and cool, finally put it out by smothering it with the sand and a blanket. Right down in the fire he was, as far as I could see.

What an odd fellow. I hadn't known him at all so far. Very generous and thought-ful. Sweet to me. And now I thought— Lucky me, not a fool in case of trouble. And I found myself being very proud of him. We insisted that the black man go to the hospital for blacks. The Belgians thought we were being rather ridiculous.

Anyway, he went. We took him. And we decided not to go back to the fishing village.

Thus passed about five days. In the afternoons, when it was too hot to do anything but nap, I went up to my room and studied the script. I must say here that this terrible thing always happens to me when I've finally decided to do a particular play or movie. I stare at it and stare at it and I begin to think that it is the most wildly boring piece of junk that I could possibly be tied up with. And I hope something awful will happen and I won't have to perform in it. Not different, *The African Queen*. Reading first a scene from the book and then one from the script. It seemed to me utterly dull and I kept falling asleep over it. What a mess.

Well, finally. The next day we were to leave for Biondo, our camp, cut out of the jungle near the Ruiki River. Betty Bogart and I had sent back to England everything but things absolutely necessary, for we could see that they would only collect mold. Especially our decent leather luggage.

By this time most of the company had pants, shirts, mosquito boots, and hats suitable for the jungle. To show the extremes of lack: Bogie was wearing my safari pants and coat, a man's suit which I had bought from Abercrombie's. A perfect fit—we just split the pants a bit down the rear seam. We packed our duds and I found myself moving all my odd stools—spears—arrows—chairs—down into the accountant's room on the first floor for him to send to New York for me. Things almost impossible to pack. A stink of a job to foist off on anyone. You remember him—the accountant—the rightful inhabitant of my third-floor room. He was most gracious about it all. How could I be so awful? Apparently easily. Lots of laundry to be done, and the houseboy had come back with it soaking wet and left it on my bed in a roll. It had rained quite a lot and they'd not been able to dry it. So I tore around and finally persuaded someone to iron it so that it wouldn't have to be packed wet.

We started off. First we crossed the Congo River to the railroad station on the other side. There we boarded the train. It was a wood-burning Toonerville Trolley. We had the private car belonging to the head of the line. There was an engine—a wood car instead of a coal car—several closed baggage cars—and three passenger cars—including ours. The Bogies'—Spiegel's—and mine. Then a number of open freight cars. I was carrying a bottle of water and some English tinned biscuits just in case there turned out to be no food. Our car had two tables, five hard armchairs, an old-fashioned icebox, a little separate alcove consisting of two beds and a john and a shower. And a porter to take care of us. It was hot as hell. We'd checked the drinks and food supposed to be there and found virtually nothing. Went tearing about and finally got some canned juice and some beer and put it in the icebox. Far too few sandwiches had been made.

Everyone waved us goodbye and off we went in a cloud of sparks. Sweat poured. Sweat poured down Sam, who weighs a ton and should sweat. And he kept mopping it up and taking showers. The shower was a rubber hose with an end fastened to the wall and a hole in the floor. It was lined with linoleum. There were two trickles of water. It was a waste of energy—you were hotter when you finished.

I sweated too, like mad. Bogie not a bit. Betty always looked beautiful. Bogie's lack of sweating seemed to me a very unhealthy sign. I anticipated his early collapse in the jungle, for I had heard that he drank quite a bit. What the hell. I'd already been with him ten days. He did drink quite a bit, but it had no effect on him as far as I could see. Either for better or for worse. He and Huston would be a great team. They drank more than plenty. I'm a great one on good habits of life, so you can imagine what went through my mind as I looked at them. Sorry pair . . .

I beg your pardon? What cigarettes do I smoke? Oh—! How could you?

While we're looking at people, let's look at Betty. I kept looking at her and looking at her. In the first place, she is young and she has lovely tawny skin and she has the most fabulous sandy hair. Beautiful whether it's straight or curled. In fact you have never seen her until you've seen her in her bright-green wrapper on the way to the outhouse in the early morning with her hair piled up on her head and no lipstick or anything else. Her sleepy-slanty green eyes and her common-sense look and her lost voice and her lanky figure and her apparent fund of pugilistic good-nature. Once she gets on the track of anything, be it picking out a can of baked beans or doing her nails or typing a letter or sunbathing or talking to anyone, don't try to get her on anything else—don't try to hurry her—she is immovable. I gazed at her and wondered whether I would go mad with jealousy as I compared our ages —our skin—our hair—our natures. No, she didn't sweat much either. She and Bogie seemed to have the most enormous opinion

Here they are—isn't she pretty?

of each other's charms, and when they fought it was with the utter confidence of two cats locked deliciously in the same cage.

The track went right through the jungle. We stopped at several stations and bought bananas. At one station a woman rushed home and made us some more sandwiches. I went with her. She'd been out there twenty-five years. At first the only white woman in the village, which consisted of nothing. Her husband was working for the government. Now they had a house with a Frigidaire, which is a wonderful luxury down there. And as a pastime her husband painted. It was a charming house: two-storied—big —neat—clean—comfortable. Wonder what happened to them in the trouble?

Off we went again. Darkness fell. We could see ourselves proceeding in a rain of wood sparks. Beautiful. The roofs of the cars kept catching on fire. The jungle never, for it is much too damp. We slept in our chairs. Or took turns on the beds. Sam and I kept taking showers. Nothing helped. Finally, eight hours later, we arrived at Ponthierville. It was about 7:00 p.m. and dark as pitch. The platform was jammed, and a little girl rushed up to me with a bunch of flowers. How she knew that I was the glamorous movie star I do not know. I wasn't even wearing lipstick. I was going to do the movie without any lipstick, and the kind I usually used left tracks—patches. My hair was slinked up under my Mexican straw sombrero and I wore a sort of white planter's costume. I looked like a very freckled female impersonator. But anyhow I got the bunch of flowers. Then the little girl rushed up to my hairdresser with the ones meant for Betty, and the hairdresser, a lively English girl, delightedly took them and thought everyone in Ponthierville most kind. The poor ladies of Ponthierville were most embarrassed, but I promised to share mine with Betty. We were whizzed into a sedan and driven away into the dark on our way to Biondo, our jungle dwelling, about forty miles away. Apparently the hurry was something about a ferry boat. I was in the front seat and the Bogies in the back. The manager of the camp—name of Geoffrey—had come to meet us. A black boy was the driver. I don't need to explain to you that John hadn't come to greet us. No, I'm sure you didn't expect it. Neither had I.

That ferry boat. That full-mooned night. The peepers at full blast. The hoot owls. The screech of an occasional monkey. The

46

ferry boat was a raft built on several huge pirogues with a ramp which let down for the cars to drive on and off. Were they wide enough? We were pulled over by a series of ropes along another rope. Very primitive and very slow. We were crossing the Ruiki River. Fifty yards wide here. And downriver from our location about twenty miles. The ramp went down and off we went onto the road on the other side. Already several cars with the rest of the company were waiting their turn to cross.

Through the jungle again. Through several tiny villages bordering big coffee plantations. Seeing nothing, really, for it was all very dark and unreal.

My mind was beginning to turn again on Huston. The end of my quest. Was he going to be interested in working on the script? As we bounced along the road, my mind fastened on my persecution in regard to the script so hard that when we very suddenly arrived at our village and turned in and drove up to the eating and main building, there he was in a pair of tan pants and a pink-checked gingham shirt smiling gaily and saying, "Hello, dear—hello, honey," to Betty and me, and to my horror I heard myself

Our car crosses the river on a raft—no bridges.

say: "What about the script?—I hope to God we're going to talk about it now!"

He looked up quickly, all joy gone out of his face and only some very thin features left. Hard and fast and dry, he said: "We'll talk about the script—honey!" And he walked over to greet Bogie.

What a lovely start. Oh hell—oh hell. Now, why did I have to bounce that out? There. Of all moments. Why? What an ass! How dumb can you get? Not even out of the car. And pick pick pick! "What about the script?" Like an old fusspot.

And no exclamation about what a wonderful job they'd done on the camp. Too late I looked about, and it *was* simply fascinating. Bamboo and palm huts.

Where is mine? "Up there—Miss Kate . . ." A man pointed into the shadows. There were two. Oh prayers, I hope mine's the one on the right. It was! Bogie's on the left. Oh boy, mine's the best, I thought to myself. Farthest away and no one at my back. Which is which, I asked, pointing N.E.S.W. No one knew. High palms north —well—lots of trees won't make too much difference to the sun.

By now I was in my hut. I opened my camera case and took out my compass. Yes.

Good. Favored E.S.W. with my porch. Quickly—quickly all this happened and I looked and took in my hut—my own rooms—my porch and my bedroom—porch opened on two sides—high bamboo railing. Low bamboo square table built into ground—three benches without backs also built into the ground surrounding table— uncomfortable, immovable. I'll swipe a real chair from somewhere with arms and back. One side of porch a solid wall—the other solid but for the door into the bedroom— other two sides railed—the whole hut a square and the porch cut out of the square —the roof overhung about two and a half feet.

Inside the bedroom. Left of door and right of door cupboards for clothes to be hung and curtained with maroon-and-yellow-striped curtains—five-foot stripes—these also in windows. I didn't care much for the colors—I wondered what the Bogies got. Also a bedspread of same on the army cot. A framework above for mosquito net. The wall on the left and the wall on the right each had a window about five feet long and two and a half feet wide. The wall opposite the door onto the porch was blank. I put my aluminum trunk under the window on the left.

Under the one on the right was a table of bamboo with an enamel basin and a pitcher. The bed was opposite the door, sticking right out from the blank wall. There was a tiny bamboo bed table. The ceiling—or the roof, rather—was pointed—the electric light hung down from the center of one point into the bedroom and the center of the other point onto the porch. The entire back side of my establishment bordered the jungle, as I was on the edge of the camp.

From the porch I had a commanding view of everything. To the right and down a bit, the Bogies. To the left and down, a men's bedroom building. And straight ahead but far enough away, the bar and eating establishment. Where was the thing? Oh yes—there it is—west, off my porch down a path—first the showers—one for the Bogies and one for me—and then, ten points farther on, the outhouses. The showers were very nice, but mud floors. I'll get some of this big bamboo as a flooring—the bamboo three to four inches in diameter placed close together—easy to stand on and good drainage. Above there was a barrel and a short pipe and a shower head. There was a chain you pulled and out came water—about a cupful. If you wanted more, you pulled again. Another cup fell out. And so on. Water was scarce. Walls and roof of bamboo and palm.

John had joined me.

"How absolutely wonderful!"

"Do you like it—honey?"

"It's just absolutely wonderful!"

A shower! I danced back down the path to the hut. My hut. It's by far the best, I thought. And the porch and the curtains. "It's absolutely great! How in the world did you ever do it? I just adore it!"

"Do you—honey? Do you, dear—do you really like it?"

I looked at him. He was eager. My face was all smiles.

I stepped right over and gave him a big warm genuine hug. "It's just perfect—I adore it—I'd like to stay forever."

Finally . . . at this moment . . . we connected . . . we sparked each other. I thought, He's like a kid. He's fixed it all up and he wants to be admired. He thought, Well—she's kind of enthusiastic—sees the good and not the bad. . . . I hoped he'd forgotten my brick about the script.

By now I even sort of liked my maroon-and-yellow-striped curtains.

We went to the Bogies'. Red-and-blue curtains and white. My favorite colors.

Ah well. But my location was far superior. What an awful brain I have—so competitive—funny. I'm not jealous about people or work, at least not compared to some. But the location of my hut? Oh, how that mattered. I'll pay anything anyone wants for a house if I like it enough. I have a passion for locations. I like to be the king of the mountain. Don't like things back of me. I was happy. I had the best location. This wasn't going to be so bad.

They had waited dinner for us. It was about ten. I hung up all my stuff. Fixed up my dressing table. Put up my pictures of Mother and Dad. Took out my big green linen pincushion with its Irish-lace cover made by my sister Peg and the Irish banshee sitting on the top. Put out my John Fredericks soap and my books and my clock and my searchlight with five batteries. Thank God for that. The electric-light situation was lousy—I could see that. The moths and bugs flew in the paneless windows. Whipped about the light bulb and dropped dead onto the mosquito net covering the bed. Yes, I thought, then they'll filter through onto me. Ah well . . . I washed my face. Suddenly I noticed the floor, for I had slopped my water, and the straw mat that I was standing

On my porch.

Tahili Bokumba provides hot water.
I wash my hair every evening.

on got slippery—and I observed that it was only a small straw mat over a *mud* floor.

Funny the things which civilization has to offer which one misses. Flooring is a lovely thing. Gives one confidence. During my five weeks' occupancy the mud floor stayed wet in spite of great care on my part not to slop the water again. It never did properly dry, because the hut was necessarily dark. No direct sun came in, and the humidity was so terrific that even in direct sunlight nothing ever dried out. Curious to live on a slippery surface. A floor is a very important item.

I took a shower. That was lovely. I had a toweling wrapper—good guess. Straw slippers—also a good guess. The water here too was soft as honey and the temperature sufficiently hot so that the cold water was most refreshing. Not bad—not bad. Put on a fresh planter's coat and pants—they're made of sharkskin—and went down the path to the bar. People. There were lots of people. I hadn't really registered who any of them were—I'm sort of slow in this respect. I strolled through the bar into the restaurant. I picked a table in the corner for the Bogies, John and me. The tables were metal and the backless seats were attached to them and they folded up. I could hear the salesman:

"So easy to ship—all one piece—table and chair." True enough. And they should be shipped and shipped and never used. If the bench wiggled, the table wobbled. And after a day's work to come back to eat dinner off of a moving object, sitting on a bench with no back, was too horrible. We moved in studio chairs and we got a new table. The guests, when they came, were given the all-in-ones.

So many strange people. We had drinks. I was not much of a drinker—at least not the way I was a smoker—but I saw that a drink come evening would be a great help in this situation. I looked about—they all looked so friendly. John and the Bogies and the English crew and all the new people of the camp—two Indians. A Belgian couple, Van Thoms, ran the camp—provided the food. If someone didn't understand English, you tried French. John didn't speak a word of French but he was learning Swahili. He had a list of words. Already he was telling a long story to someone. Betty was listening to a long story from someone. Bogie was sitting seemingly quite content and relaxed with no one. There was a monkey named Romulus.

OVERLEAF: A moment of peace.

He became the center of attention. He was in Betty's lap. I don't particularly like monkeys. He leaped about and bit people and drank their drinks. Everyone howled. I tried to join in. But it just seemed to me entirely stupid. Maybe I'd be better off if I . . . Glory be—this was going to be awful. Well, I would be able to escape after dinner.

Finally we went in to eat—I say "finally." Dinner was announced. I gave a look at John. He was still telling his story and didn't hear it—or he didn't care. I hung around and hung around. Oh God, those stories. I don't know how many words came out a minute—but articulation with this genius is a real problem and he's so concentrated that nothing throws him. He doesn't even seem aware of whether anyone is listening. He walks the same way, cleans a gun the same way, and they say he reads in the bathtub. He takes absolutely forever to make up his mind to do anything and forever to do it. "Go on in, honey—I'll be right there." How many times was I to hear this? Well— oh goddamn—goddamn. But actually what's the matter with you, Kath? Pick up a magazine and go on in. You may have more privacy than you thought.

Next came Bogie. Next came Betty.

Last came John. First left Bogie. Next left Betty. Last—eat and eat—John and me. During the first dinner there, when I was sitting alone, I thought to myself—Now— *honey!* It's cruel that you are *not* going to change him. Yes, you may be set in your ways too, but you are not anywhere near as set as he is. Better change away. It will pay. And—anyhow—you may find out that there is something to another way of living.

The food was excellent, incidentally. The couple named Van Thoms were responsible. They were cooking for fifty people. They had a four-burner bottled-gas stove—two ovens and a series of wood fires all over the mud floor of a fair-sized tent—each fire run by a black who was burning his fingers while doing toast on the end of a fork or this or that. The place so filled with smoke that your eyes wept. Very hot. We would have a little tasty cheese on tomato or something. Then the meat course and potatoes and two vegetables. A homemade dessert. Then coffee—this was the only bad thing—too weak. And wine with all. It was a triumph. How Madame Van Thoms did it I will never know. She practically had a nervous breakdown before the end but she never let us know. How wonderful are the women and men in the world who feed us. Especially those who feed us with no salary. The mothers— I thought. The wives. My work is so delicious. Always different, and people go to the trouble of writing about it. My God—here I am in Africa and someone else footing the bills. How could I be so lucky? But the average family has food at least two times a day and, for quite a number, seven days a week. It's an endless chain and usually complaints or no comment and taken for granted.

So dinner. We talked of this and that. Mainly hunting. We were to begin work day after tomorrow. By then all the crew would be present. We were lacking a wardrobe woman, so I was taking care of the costumes for the moment. The script wasn't mentioned. I went to bed. John escorted me to my hut and we said goodnight. I went to bed and had a wonderful sleep. Straw mattress—straw pillow—a sheet for covering. It was very cozy. Tomorrow I would fix the lighting system, then everything would be fine. I could hear the noise from the bar and the Victrola, but it did not bother.

Next morning was a lovely day. I took a shower and went down to the general hut and got a tray and collected breakfast. Slow work as always, the first arrangements. Sliced

fresh pineapple—toast—coffee—marmalade
—an egg now and then—hard to get—and
grilled ham, not very good. Took it back to
the porch of my hut. Was one of the earliest
risers as usual. I stole a chair from the bar
and ate tilted back against the porch wall
with my feet on the bamboo table, gazing
out into the impenetrable jungle. Had a
pillow in my lap and the tray on the pillow.
Very close to breakfast in bed.

The camp manager—Geoffrey Dunes—
came by and introduced me to my personal
"boy"—mine! Tahili Bokumba. He spoke
and understood a little French. So did I.
We did not always mean the same thing by
the same thing, but he was a hard worker—
an excellent launderer and he finally caught
on to breakfast—always the same and on a
tray and on the porch. Five pails of very hot
water which must be clean and heated on my
petrol stoves (brilliant purchase) and not over
a wood fire—and thus filled with sparks and
dirt and smelling of smoke. This water I had
to have every evening between five-thirty and
seven, when we quit work, so that I could
wash my hair. It took me the better part of
a week to get this straight. Rotate the pots.
He was eager and helpful. Keep all hot.

We both liked flowers and we had some

very Constance Spry–ish arrangements in fruit jars and stuck into the palm wall of my porch. Lovely strange leaves. We even had an orchid given to me by a Belgian coffee planter who came to visit—he lived ten miles down the road. When we came there, in late May and June, most of the flowers had already bloomed. Tahili and I hit it off from the start. You can't be impatient and you must make a joke. He liked to smoke, so I gave him cigarettes and matches. He took excellent care of me. I was lucky. He tried to teach me Swahili and I tried to teach him French. Neither succeeded. We were both rather stupid.

We looked about the camp, then drove down through the tiny group of huts which constituted the village of Biondo. Goats and children swarmed over the road. They waved madly as we drove by, shouting, *"Jambo"* —which means "hello"—to our *"Jambo."* When they wave they hold both arms straight out, palm toward you, and turn the palm left to right—right to left; they don't flap it up and down as we do. Later, in perfect English, they would wave the same way but shout, "O.K.—O.K." Which now means, in Biondo, in the Congo, "Hello." Always all these greetings were accompanied with screams of laughter. On both our parts.

In Biondo there was a priest. He had a tiny chapel and a schoolhouse. I used to have long talks with him while I walked to and fro from the location at the Ruiki River. He said that he did his best to teach them to read and write and to learn a bit of French. He said that he usually lost them to life between the ages of fourteen and thirty. Then, exhausted, they would return to school. And to God. But he persisted. The gain seemed minuscule but he persisted. He was their solace in time of despair. These individuals did such noble jobs—in human terms. Then came the trouble.

The Ruiki River is small. Sixty feet wide and curving and very black water. Beautiful reflections of the lush green banks.

The first location was for the burial of Robert Morley. One of John's "finds," about two and a half miles up the river. For a vehicle to take us there, we had the *African Queen*. A thirty-foot metal hull with a thirty-year-old engine and a huge boiler and a fake steam pump. We also had the administrator's launch. A very top-heavy motor craft with an inside cabin in which you could not stand upright. It held ten people in a squeeze.

Aft of this, in a two-foot space, stood the boy with the tiller. Amidships you stood still or crawled aft on hands and knees and down a ladder into the cabin . . . or forward into the engine cabin. An agony of inconvenience, but it became my dressing room. There were windows either side—three of them. To open you pushed one side and the other side went inside. Also a window aft. Seats along either side. Remember, you couldn't stand straight. It was, as you see, divided into four sections—all most difficult of entry. To have privacy you had to close all the windows to close the curtains. Never forget the day it filled with tsetse flies. We went through swarms. The boys at the tiller dived through the aft window into the cabin. Vi Murray— the wardrobe girl—was with us by then, thank God. She used to say—she had a great nature—"Not to worry, but if to worry, not to worry unduly." But this day she worried plenty.

You kept gouging yourself if the windows were open. We had a filthy chemical toilet and a six-foot-by-eighteen-inch mirror which had already been chipped. That mirror—that bloody mirror—I'll tell you about that later. . . . Oh, what the hell—may as well now— might forget. Well, I wanted a mirror—and

Eileen Bates watches while I put on my hat.

I wanted a mirror in which I could see, really see, in order to work fast. There I was stuck with Bogie and Huston—two over-male men. Well, I had an over-male father and I certainly didn't have to work with either of them to find out that waiting for me, a female, to do my hair, fix my makeup or get dressed—in short, to titivate—would seem highly unreasonable. As the climate was one hundred percent humidity, and as my hair is very fine and straight as a string, I lived in hair curlers. I make them out of rolled-up newspapers, in different sizes according to the location on my head. This not even necessarily to curl my hair, in this case only to give it body. Luckily I have lots of it. Hair, I mean. Well, you can imagine. With the damp I'd take it down and in no time it would be straight as a string. So to anticipate I would roll it up immediately after a scene. I never have a permanent, for it makes it feel funny, it makes it smell, and I'm a sort of impractical character. Love the feeling of soft, clean hair. Can't remember that anyone ever made a comment, certainly not either of these jerks. But please yourself and at least someone is pleased.

But as I say. Doing my hair up and down and up and down and dressing and undress-

The mirror at the beginning of its career.

ing and making up, it was a relief—nay, a necessity—to have a big mirror. Everyone squalled about this mirror. But Vi Murray, the wardrobe girl; Eileen Bates, the hairdresser; George Frost, the makeup man, and I paid them no mind and carried it along. It was just too long to fit across the back of the floor of the car, so we rode along with the car door slightly ajar. Daily it had to be taken from my hut to the car. Downhill to the boat. To the jungle. Back to the boat. Up the hill into the car again with the door open. To my hut. It had no backing. Finally it broke being put into the car—one-third broke off. Everyone was glad. That's the end of that, they thought. But we carried it anyway. Now with a great jagged end. But now the car door would close. And everyone used it. Oh yes, especially Bogie. And everyone crabbed. Life—life.

Anyway, this administrator's launch was our second means of conveyance. It was forty feet long. And it always felt that it was about to roll over.

There was an empty hull into which went the generator.

There was a huge raft, say fifteen, eighteen feet, made of wood and built on five pirogues. It carried separate sections (called mock-ups) of the *African Queen:* the back seat and tiller—the spot where Bogie stood against the boiler—the place where Bogie stoked the boiler. These were used when they wanted to get close to us. It enabled them to surround us with necessary equipment. The raft also carried our equipment and the two lights. It had to be dragged behind the boat. And it was quite a thing to tow us and all our stuff the two and a half miles to the location and back again at night.

The local blacks didn't know what in the world we were trying to do. They were supposed to fill out our insufficient crew. But it was almost hopeless, as they couldn't understand our language. Nor could we theirs. I'm sure it seemed to them utterly idiotic. Lugging stuff up the river—getting dressed up—sitting around—sitting in the *African Queen*—talking gibberish—taking little trips —and doing it over and over again—then going home. And doing the same thing again the next day. They thought we were crazy. They'd never seen a movie. Or maybe they had. . . .

So . . . the day after we got there was lovely and we examined the situation. We planned to shoot Morley's burial. . . . He was in London playing in *The Little Hut*. We had a double. Anyway, we were burying him, so he didn't show. I had asked him why he—a big London star—should be willing to play such a lousy part, and he said: "Oh—darling—I think it would be rather fun to play your brother." Then I had asked him whether he'd read the script and he said, "Most of it"—very casual. He has a great time and is such a good actor that he makes anything he plays seem delicious.

Our first working day:

Dawn broke—rather, it didn't. It was raining. I was sitting eating my breakfast, delighted. I love rain. It's lucky, I always think—and I dreaded actually starting the picture. And the bloody script—maybe now we'd go over it. The raindrops pelted down, making wonderful sounds on the palm trees and on the roof. It made everything seem very cozy. And as I looked out at the mud I thought: Well, certainly not today. Saw the Bogies begin to stir. . . . "Morning . . . dear," said Bogie—all tousled—hair standing on end—terrible old wrapper—wandering over to the outhouse. He looked neither right nor left. Then back he came. Looked up at the black sky. "Great!" he said. And went around the corner back to his hut. I hoped his coffee would be waiting for him. . . .

Every morning, ditto.

Then Betty in her green robe . . . I've already told you about her. And on her way back—just before she rounded the corner— she looked up at the black sky. "God!" she muttered. I saw their breakfast tray going toward their hut.

John lived down near the office—he had a noisy spot, but a shower connected with his hut. I never did see him go to the outhouse. Maybe he never did. Wouldn't surprise me a bit. Would explain a great deal.

Not enough light in his room. Lucky he was tall.

The camp slowly came to life. I knew which ones showered in the morning—all about them. And every morning each one did the same things. It was fascinating to observe what creatures of habit we are. The morning grouchies—the morning happies. Down by the men's barracks on my left they put their small standing mirrors on the edge of the thatched roof to shave—the tall ones. That was a funny sight—rain or shine. Inside it was too dark to see. Our electric lights only worked at night. The ladies in a long line with pails of water on their heads appeared, and the men took the pails and filled the barrels over the showers. What a grand spot I had. I sipped my coffee and I wrote letters and I peeked at everything and everyone. Just love this hour of the day. Heaven to be the first one up and to eat breakfast all alone. I sat in my big toweling wrapper with my hair all rolled up in curlers—it had to be up all night, for we had no hair dryer. Stuck it up soaking wet for dinner and then rolled it up just before I went to bed.

I've been stalling along here because I wonder whether I should go into the morning problem frankly or just avoid it. Bowels are not exactly a polite subject for conversation, but they are certainly a common problem, and I know we wondered exactly what would go on in regard to this. Please think of me again as the urologist's daughter. As you may recall, I had protected myself with a pot in case of trouble. This pot was the lower half of an aluminum double boiler. In case of discovery it might be anything. Well, it might be the lower half of an aluminum double boiler. I saw the Siamese-twin outhouse for the Bogies and me and my heart sank. For though I expected to be very intimate with them—I did feel that sitting there together in the early morning would be going a bit further than the ordinary demands of co-starring in a motion picture. The question was, when would he make the trip? I can only say that after a few visits—to my horror—I would hear his palm door open (you can't hear anyone coming down a mud path). And I would leap up and out. This would never do. Must be practical. So I resorted to privacy and my pot. I was old enough to have had some early farm experience with pots and was on to lining it with newspapers. Very clean and neat . . . Then when I could see that the coast was clear I would ostensibly go to take a shower with many bath towels covering my lower half of the double boiler, quickly dispose of it and rush for the shower. A very excellent solution to this problem. It may disgust you that I have brought it up at all, but who knows? Life has some problems which are basic for all of us—and about which we have a natural reticence. And some day you may find this information very useful. The toilet is an excellent thing. The outhouse is an agony. The pot—well—a poor thing—but your own.

So a lovely shower and back to my porch. John is a late riser. As late as possible—in fact, later. He used to be seen meandering around in his old blue pajamas and drinking a cup of coffee here and a cup of tea there. He came to my porch only once for breakfast. I said: "John, I like to eat breakfast alone. I like to think and read and write and contemplate—I always feel great when I wake up, and I don't like idle conversation at that hour." I liked idle conversation with only one, I should say—and he wasn't there. I speculated as to whether or not to be honest and then I said: "I like to be alone at breakfast." "Oh" . . . and off he went and he never came again. I don't think he gave a damn and it really did matter a lot to me. But if he did, he certainly never let on. He has respect for others' oddities.

So the first working day was a rainy day.

And the second and the third—constant rain. I filled my porch with flowers and leaves. It was charming and I sat. John came ambling up late morning of the first day with his script. And by the third day we'd gone through most of it. He would argue and Bogie would come by. Suspicious of me. For the male star has a natural suspicion of a female star who is interested in script changes. But he discovered quickly that my interest was general, not personal. . . . We had long and amiable arguments—nothing much was done, really, and I seemed to be happy. I found that I could be quite honest with John about what I thought, and I also found that where I had good ideas he would take them. Where I was just worrying and confusing the issue, he would say, "Let it alone." The whole thing of the script seemed less and less important. We got to talking about all sorts of things. . . . I have a reputation for being highly intellectual—something about my manner and the shape of my face. Or I am confused with the reputation of my father or mother. Actually I am quick, but not much memory and not really well informed. I could always get by. John, on the other hand, has read everything under the sun and remembers most of it. And loves to talk and discuss. I like to do this too. The hours passed—delightfully. He tells me the most wonderful long stories.

What am I saying? Is this the same man? Well, I promised to tell you the truth. True, he's a bit slow getting them out. But he has a kind of lanky charm and he inherited enough of Walter's showmanship so that he's fun. He has a ridiculous but distinguished face. Very fine hair . . . dark dark brown and a few gray . . . wants to curl. A small head or, rather, a small face. Flat, pointed ears like Pan. His hair is always too long about the edges. Thin Irish skin. Black deepset eyes. Black beetle-brows and two long hairs straying out of the left one. His nose is pointed and quite nostriled. And the nose was hit in a boxing match and was broken, so the top is squashed down a bit and the end pushed up. His mouth is neither thin nor full nor large nor small but seems now one, now the other, according to his moods. He laughs a lot. He has wonderful even teeth—very white and with a brown speck on one of the big front ones. The lower ones are apt to be tobacco-stained. His face is quite lined. He has a noble chin. He has a very thin neck . . . is definitely of the bird family. He's very tall and skinny.

John with his real love.

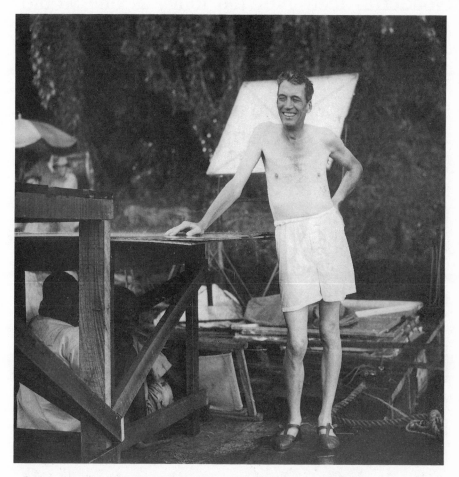

John is happy. Perhaps he never looked down.

His chest caves in and his stomach sticks out. Stands—sits—lies in a stooped position. Never breathes. His strong wrists and strong smooth hands are like a young boy's. And wonderful feet. Not too long, as one would expect in someone so tall. Fine ankles. His voice is very pleasant. He uses long words and mispronounces plenty of them. He speaks with an Ohio accent. He is very personable. Full of charm, conscious and unconscious. He likes to live. When he was sitting on the porch in the rain, he was getting all that one can possibly get out of sitting on that porch in the rain. Then we would talk about the script again—and we'd talk about the characters. It was fun.

They were very full days, those days, with the rain pelting down, and Sam Spiegel, who bore the financial responsibility, was going mad trying to find out whether or not he had been misinformed about which was the rainy season. He had housed us at Claridge's —he had furnished us each with a Rolls-Royce and driver. He had sent us caviar and champagne. Being a Connecticut Yankee, I was aware of this lavish expenditure and suggested to Sam that I would be very happy living on a slightly lower scale—

He was shocked.

Never—the best is none too good.

I watched him in his shorts and colored shirts rushing around that camp in the rain—and I thought: Alone alone alone. The man who has to pay the bills—terrifying.

Sam is an extraordinary man. He is a real impresario, in the true sense of the word. Has an eye for an "occasion" and can "get it together." The script—the girl—the man —the director—the unique presentation—the sell. Not easy. Try it. Always overcoming negative reaction. He got the ball rolling on *African Queen* in spite of no money—no nothing. Like rolling a number of hoops. And all at the same time—Oops—hit that one. Excuse me—hit this one. Just don't let them stop. Don't let them escape. And, of course, any producer is the recipient of every complaint. He has a sharp mind. And a deep well of energy. And a sort of a great sense of "Isn't this the greatest idea you ever heard of?" I liked him. He loves his work and he loves life. He's a doer. This was the beginning of his extraordinary run of lovely pictures. His now very full purse was then nonexistent. But somehow he kept things moving ahead.

Incidentally, I never did hear the same

thing from anyone about this rainy-season business. It reminded me of California's Chamber of Commerce explaining away bad California weather: "Very unseasonable. Never saw it this way before." We slid everywhere in the mud, but my spirit was good, for I thought this long string bean of a director isolated with us in the jungle was not going to be too hard to handle.

I had a chance to walk from our own camp to the village of Biondo and to inspect the little Catholic mission church. It was indeed a haven of rest and faith and of teaching there in the jungle. The priest was very poor and he worked very hard. He had the church and next door the school. He taught them to read and to write Swahili. The lack of education is terrifying and the enormity of the problem beyond the comprehension of someone not versed in these things. There was a black Chief—Sultani Paul—who ruled over the black men in the district we were in. He was a fine-looking man, tall and well built. His word was law as to when—where —and how the natives should work. He lived most of the time in Ponthierville. He spoke some French, so he could converse with us fairly comfortably.

Ordinarily he wore a sort of tropical Navy

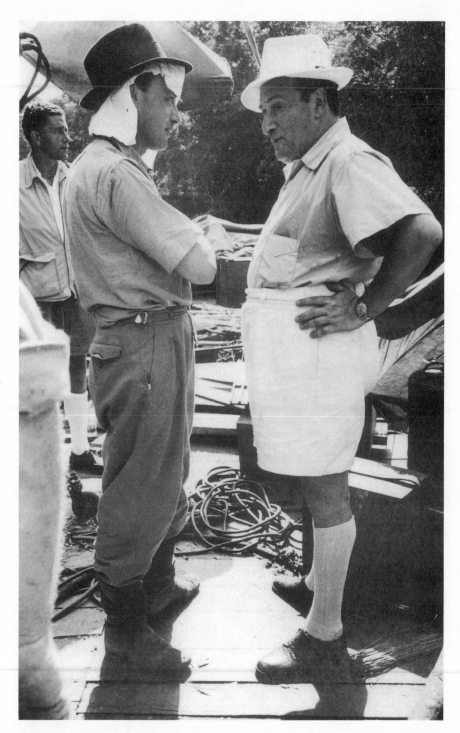

Sam Spiegel may be losing money, but he's not *yet* losing
weight. Jack Cardiff listens.

The Methodists get a steeple and a cross. Sam figures the cost.

uniform. His native dress was a wonderful headdress of feathers and turkey-red material made into a very odd pair of bloomers tied and draped up. Then some metal decorations and a short dagger with a very fancy handle. He was most kind to us and also most helpful. He was very much more husky and well filled out than his subjects. It was easy to see that a good diet makes all the difference. For he is a rich man. It was hard for me at first to tell one black from another, just as I am sure that we confused them. As they became friends, naturally they looked totally individual.

My first personal recognition of my helper, Tahili, was his running off on some errand for me, and he was very short-legged in comparison to his body and was slightly crippled—so that as he moved away he seemed to take a few steps, then put in a little hop. He hurried. His arms and neck and shoulders were strong and he had a good head. But thin little wretched legs. This was a common thing. Blue eyes were common too. . . . Tahili had a very black skin, as most of the natives do—eyes far apart, a common and very attractive characteristic—medium snub nose—fairly but not very prominent lips and chin and good teeth. He had a funny habit of looking down on the ground when he was embarrassed and laughing and sort of pawing on the ground with his bare foot. Stalling to see how things were going. Rolling his eyes. He was so warmhearted and so anxious to do well and so eager to find out something new every day so that he could lord it over his friends. I had a map on the wall and we studied it with fascination. I wonder if he knew what I meant and what the map meant. . . . The minute he saw that I liked to arrange flowers for my hut, he did it too. He would fix up all my shelves. He would rearrange my pocketbook—this he adored to do. I carry all sorts of things in an old leather bag. One day I came home and he had the entire contents spread out on the floor. I'd been to a lot of places, so I had a big variety of monies and pens and pencils and little notebooks and hard candies and postcards, lipsticks and swatches of material and pictures and a St. Christopher and a small ivory Alaskan seal—a little red folding book—passport and papers, etc. He was sitting on the mat surrounded with these things. I knew just how he felt—Grandma's trunk. There was a tiny case with a pen and pencil in gold—I think it had been sent out by the Stork Club. Years ago I went there once and ever since then they have sent the most glamorous things. Ads, I suppose they are, but I always open their packages with much excitement.

Anyway, Tahili was gazing at the pen and pencil. I gave them to him. Then he would brush all the loose tobacco out of the bag and put everything back. He never took a match without asking me. Some days he would be in a sort of decline and unable to work. Just the misery of life, and his eyes would look very worried. He could never really explain to me what was wrong, for we had such a limit of words which we understood in common. He would often borrow writing paper and envelopes and write letters. I think he had a fascinating wife in Stanleyville. Sometimes I'd be sitting at the bar at night and I'd hear a voice far off in the dusk: *"Madame—Madame—allumettes!"* And I'd steal the matches off the bar and stroll out with them. He was a dear man. I hated to leave him behind. He came with us to Uganda when we went—got a ride over on one of our trucks. Train travel was a bit of a problem for the blacks in those days. He was let in on a temporary work permit as being indispensable to me. Hippity-hop down the path he'd go, his black feet between the

path railings so whitewashed. Hurrying—
hurrying—but where? My God, where and
for what?

It's hard to say anything about the natives
and whether they work hard and how they
were treated and what was their situation
here or there. It goes from good to bad. As
we go—as they go. There are tremendous
problems of which we have not the vaguest
comprehension. Then or now. A real lack of
education is a tough thing to combat. And
the country is so big and transportation is
so difficult. It's tough too on the whites who
moved out there to supposedly earn a for-
tune on coffee. They had paid a tremendous
price and lost. The country is like a great
sponge—it finally absorbs you. Eventually
you will get malaria or you will get dysen-
tery and whatever you do, if you don't keep
doing it, the jungle will grow over you. Black
or white, you've got to fight it every minute
of the day.

The day was clear—we started work. This
meant that the five autos and trucks carried
us in loads the three and a half miles through
Biondo to the edge of the Ruiki River. There
we unloaded everything. Carried it down the
hill onto the raft or onto the *Queen* or onto
the administrator's launch. Then we went by

these boats two and a half miles or so up the river to our working location. There we unloaded the first day, as we were to shoot on land. The rest of the time we were shooting on the *Queen* or on the various fake parts of the *Queen* which had been built on the raft —the "mock-ups," as I said before. It was easier to photograph us this way, as the Technicolor camera was huge and we needed lights and reflectors and with sound we have to have a lot of room and a lot of people. If we were doing a shot on the raft where the boat was supposedly moving, the raft would be towed by the administrator's launch and the *African Queen*. As I've explained, the Ruiki River is very curving—the raft very unwieldy—a big square. When the raft was towed too fast, the pirogues underneath used to fill up with water and we'd start to sink. Or we'd be going around a curve and the raft would not follow around the curve but would continue in a straight line toward the bank and its dense overhanging foliage. John would scream—Bogie and I would jump —and the boiler would be tipped over, or nearly. The canopy would be torn off. The camera or lamps or whatever was caught by the overhanging shrubbery on the banks. Or we would be going along nicely—hit a submerged log and catch on it. Or the sun would go in. Or it would rain. The hysteria of each shot was a nightmare. And there was always the uncertain factor of Bogie and me and whether John thought we'd done a scene well. Or the engine on the *Queen* would stop. Or one of the propellers would be fouled by the dragging rope. Or we would be attacked by hornets. Or a stray pirogue would suddenly appear in the shot. If it was a stationary shot there were many of the same problems but also the question of whether the sound had picked up the generator noise. Technical problems galore and no chairs—no dressing rooms—no toilet—hot ginger ale and fruit juice and beer—the problem of sending out lunch for forty people. This became Betty Bogart's department and a wonderful job she did. But the lunch might be very late, for we had to send one of our two launches down to pick it up and often needed them in the shot. Sometimes when we were working in the middle of the stream we couldn't tie up for hours. The men solved this problem with great ease—but it was a bit tough on the ladies. . . .

However—

Making *The African Queen* was great fun. John Huston—Bogie and Betty and Peter—

were great fun to be with. And the location in Africa was a first for all of us.

The temperature in both Uganda and the Belgian Congo is always about eighty to eighty-five degrees. Almost on the Equator. Nothing ever dried.

The weather is beautiful. A clear blue sky which can cloud over very quickly in a most ominous fashion. And it pours rain. To hell with the actors. Protect the camera! Protect the sound! Then just as suddenly—it will clear. It will shine. And, having scurried for shelter, we would unscurry ourselves and get on with the work. But unfortunately the ground, after a rain, was immediately soft mud.

Now, speaking of mud—the very first scene to be shot was burying my brother—the preacher—Robert Morley—on a hillside. I hesitated. . . . Remember, I was still the wardrobe woman. Vi Murray wouldn't arrive until the third day of shooting.

The clothes I carried in an aluminum trunk, and then hung them on hangers on whatever tree was available.

OVERLEAF AND FOLLOWING PAGES: We work. We work. We work. And we rest.

Yes, Bogie, of course . . . But listen to this.

"Kneel down, dear," said John Huston.

"I'll be filthy," I answered.

"Yes, dear—kneel down—I think it would be a good idea if you knelt down next to the grave and planted a rose."

Good grief, I thought.

He had decided to bury Robert in the most difficult spot, all the way up a hill—slip—slip—slide up it—down it. The front of the linen skirt—a light light washed-out tan—would get mud on it. What a mess. Fool directors. Impractical to a moronic degree.

"What are you going to do about that hat brim, Katie?"

"What?"

"Fix the hat brim, dear—it's dipping. It's covering your face."

"Yes," I answered, "but it's the damp that's dipping it—it's losing its shape and . . ."

"Yes, that's what I mean. Fix it," he said.

I looked at the makeup man, George Frost. "What can we do?"

"Starch?"

"Are you kidding? Where?"

Yes, where? I thought. I thought.

"I know—rice water—sticky— Just a minute, John."

George and I headed for the jungle—we could see smoke rising from somewhere— a hut? Yes. We knocked—went in—there it was, the inevitable pot of rice boiling away— the basic diet of the Congo. We pointed— held out money—bought it—we let it boil low and sticky, then patted the liquid into the brim. By now the sun was out again—we let the hat dry. It worked! Down the hill we ran.

"John, it works! The brim is stiff! Hurry!"

We got the shot. Buried Morley without a ruffle. Fine day's work. I took the clothes back to the camp and the mud brushed out so that you noticed nothing. After that when I was wearing the hat we carried rice. And —thank heaven, the wardrobe woman, Vi Murray, had finally arrived. She did have to work under very primitive conditions, heating her iron by filling it with hot coals. The material of which my suit was made was a heavy sort of fake linen. It never showed the dirt. You could not tell whether it was wet or dry. Brilliant Doris Langley Moore. A great designer. Just as important—she had common sense.

The eating of lunch. I had a can with a top. In it I carried a cut-up pineapple. I opened the can. Bees would swarm from nowhere. I'd leave the can with dripping around the top and move off about fifty feet and eat my slice while the bees had their sip. I did this not because of the food—that was O.K. But the dish problem gave me pause. I saw them wash off the dishes in the Ruiki and hand them to the new customer. I eat things unwashed. And I eat things which have dropped on the floor. But here I thought twice. Stick to the pineapple and English tinned biscuits and cookies.

I had no dressing room. To change, if the administrator's launch wasn't handy, I'd go off into the trees. And for the bathroom, Betty and I would go off into the trees. Often pursued by the curious natives, whom we would shoo away. Finally I thought I really should have a decent dressing room. They built me a hut on its own private raft. But dragging it, a square, up the river proved to be totally impractical—That Katie! After a few times it was abandoned.

The only horror after the first day's work, besides the difficulty of getting up the river to the location, the hat and the minor personal discomforts, was the discovery on the second day of work that we didn't have sufficient cable to keep the generator boat far enough upriver so that we couldn't hear it.

It had to be at least three bends away unless the *Queen*'s engine was covering it. This caused no worry to John, but it nearly gave Sam a stroke. I don't blame him. John and saving money didn't mix. John was happy to wait for cable—gave him time to use his hunting license. What an irresponsible child —poor Sam.

It was during this pause that John came one morning to my hut.

"May I have a cup of coffee?"

"Yes, of course—what?"

"Well—I don't want to influence you. But incidentally . . . that was great, that scene, burying Robert. And of course you had to look solemn—serious. . . . Yes, of course—you were burying your brother. You were sad. But, you know, this is an odd tale—I mean, Rosie is almost always facing what is for her a serious situation. And she's a pretty serious-minded lady. And I wondered—well—let me put it this way— have you by any chance seen any movies of—you know—newsreels—of Mrs. Roosevelt—those newsreels where she visited the soldiers in the hospitals?"

"Yes, John—yes—I saw one. Yes."

"Do you remember, Katie dear, that lovely smile—?"

Me in my luxurious jungle dressing room.

"Yes, John—yes—I do."

"Well, I was wondering. You know, thinking ahead of our story. And thinking of your skinny little face—a lovely little face, dear. But skinny. And those famous hollow cheeks. And that turned-down mouth. You know—when you look serious—you do look rather—well, serious. And it just occurred to me—now, take Rosie—you know—you are a very religious—serious-minded—frustrated woman. Your brother just dead. Well, now, Katie—you're going to go through this whole adventure before the falls and before love raises its . . . Well, you know what I mean—solemn."

"Then I thought of how to remedy that. She's used to handling strangers as her brother's hostess. And you 'put on' a smile. Whatever the situation. Like Mrs. Roosevelt—she felt she was ugly—she thought she looked better smiling—so she . . . Chin up. The best is yet to come—onward ever onward. . . . The society smile."

A long pause.

"You mean—yes—I see. When I pour out the gin I—yes—yes—when I . . ."

"Well," he said, getting up to go. He'd planted the seed. "Think it over. . . . Perhaps it might be a useful . . ."

. . . And I listened.

He was gone.

I sat there.

That is the goddamnedest best piece of direction I have ever heard. Now, let's see. . . .

Well, he's just told me exactly how to play this part. Oh-h-h-h-h, lovely thought. Such fun. I was his from there on in.

He may have no common sense—he may be irresponsible and outrageous. But he *is* talented. He ain't where he is for no reason.

And you'd better watch him. And learn a few things.

Days passed without rain and without any real hitch. All the scenes going downriver in the earlier part of the story were shot here on the Ruiki. They just seemed to fall into place. It was a relief when the boat was still. Then we could work fast.

We'd drive in cars to the Ruiki River. Everyone would carry their own junk and whatever else they could down the hill to the boats. Pile in—go upstream. Tempers were beginning to get a bit short. One fool used to carry a shotgun with him and shoot at the gibbons who used to sit screeching at us from the treetops. He was the mechanic who took care of the engine on the *Queen*—as it was the only engine we had, it was important. One of the sound men took a wild exception to this shooting (as did most of us). There was an ugly scene. Many unforgivable things were said. Off went the mechanic. Back to Stanleyville.

"Who cares. We're rid of the pig!"

"Well—one engine . . ."

"Who cares! Good riddance!"

The happy group continued the day.

Two days later. Early morning—I was eating my breakfast in comfort. Tahili had been given an egg. And he gave it to me. A tiny little egg. A wee wee egg. But it was a treat. It *was* an egg. I was enjoying this when I saw John coming up my path. What goes on, I thought.

"May I disturb you for just a moment, dear?"

"Yes, John. Please . . ."

"May I sit?"

"Yes, John."

"The *Queen* has sunk."

"What!!"

"The *Queen* is at the bottom of the Ruiki."

"No."

"Yes."

"I don't believe . . . What about the man who was guarding it?"

"Well . . . apparently he was asked what he did when he discovered the leak. And he said with simple honesty, 'I got off.' Anyway, she's at the bottom. Just the top of the boiler showing."

"Well, what are we going to do?"

"We're going to get her up."

Everyone in the camp got going and went down to the Ruiki. There was the *Queen*. Sunk.

First, let me describe. The river here was about thirty to forty feet across. The far side was jungle. Luckily on that far side there was a big tree with a big branch sticking out almost horizontally and at a height of about twelve feet. They got a rope around the boiler, which was cast iron and heavy. Then they put the rope around this branch and brought it back to our side of the river. Then all of us—and whatever villagers were there (and they were all there, laughing away: "Oh-hah!— The whities —they're a scream . . .") — got hold of the rope. We tugged and tugged. Finally we got the boiler out of the *Queen* and up on the other bank. With the main weight out of her, the *Queen* surfaced and we had to bail her out. It took two days. Mud mud mud. Dried her out. Got the motor off. Found the insulted mechanic. Got him back from Stanleyville. He mended the motor. Got the *Queen* plugged. Got the boiler back to the *Queen*. And again we were in business.

Back home we went, full of delight that the *Queen* was back in service. I was standing inside my hut talking to Tahili—trying to explain in French what had happened—he was in the doorway. All of a sudden, I felt some itching on my ankles. I reached down

OVERLEAF: Pulling the boiler out of the sunken *Queen*.

and scratched. I went on talking—reached down again and happened to look at the mud floor. I was standing in a procession of ants—about six inches wide and an inch and a half deep. I nearly fainted. They were climbing in the window which was toward the jungle—crossing my cabin—crawling over or past me—going to the wall opposite—crawling up the wall—and going out the window on the camp side.

I tore off my clothes. I was literally covered up to my neck with ants—bitten everywhere except hands and neck and face. Those army ants crossed our campsite in as straight a line as possible, and—luckily for us—they went out the other side. Had they decided to stay—it's *we* who would have had to move. As I was wearing high necks and long sleeves, my bites didn't show.

Most of the scenes which we were to shoot on the Ruiki were now done. We finished what was left and were ready to make the move back to Ponthierville, where we were going to shoot a few close shots back of a big Congo riverboat which had a wheel at the stern. It churned up the water and gave a good semblance of Rosie and Charlie going down rapids.

We were to go to Ponthierville by car, do

the close-ups, then by train back to Stanley-ville. One more night in the Pourquoi Pas, then fly to Entebbe. The train was to leave Ponthierville at midnight.

We got to Ponthierville, changed into our costumes on the big riverboat and got into the *Queen* and churned along back of the riverboat with the spray covering us. It didn't take too long. Then we were free until the train left.

Ponthierville was a quite charming town. On the Congo. A big dock and lots of commerce going south. It rose up from the banks of the river and commanded a pretty view downriver—little shops—nice houses. A comfortable place to live.

In Ponthierville was a church which had been built by the monks—sort of mud plas-ter and palm lath, mud-colored—on the edge of town. It was very pretty and quite big. It stood at the end of a rather long—call it avenue. Also on the avenue was a nunnery, down a bit from the church. The monks had taken the responsibility of making sev-eral half-sized *African Queens*. The nuns were making the half-sized Charlies and Rosies to fasten into the boats. The boats would be put into the falls above Ponthierville and guided as long as possible as they tumbled over the falls. Teddy Scaife, the second cameraman on the picture, was to get all this stuff.

I was curious to see the church and the nunnery. And to examine the town. There was also the question of feeding all of us —we were about fifty strong. Betty undertook the responsibility for this task. Set up a sort of kitchen and bought stuff and tried to enlist me as part of her staff.

Well, I thought to myself, where's John? I bet he's not going to be wasting his few hours in this village running a catering service. Everyone's too fat anyway. No, I said. I'm not going to help. I'm going to wander. And off I went.

"Don't miss the train!" called Betty with a touch of sarcasm. Very wicked I felt. But— well—let each one fend for himself or herself. Eat a loaf of bread. A bar of chocolate. We're only here for a few hours. Live!

I wandered out the main avenue toward the monks' church. This was about three-quarters of a mile away. A bit uphill and on the edge of town. On the way there was the nunnery. Quite high walls lined the avenue. Plaster—mud-colored—sometimes painted white. Great vines growing over them. Just opposite the nunnery was the nuns' cemetery, and over the neatly trimmed and painted wall hung huge wild-looking proteas. Have you ever seen them? — Weird furry petals, pink and black-edged and white, formed like an artichoke. Very voluptuous. I went in through the gate and stood thinking by the sweet gravestones. Lives of total service. What became of them later, during the massacres . . . ? I am not in any sense a Catholic, but one couldn't help being moved by the dedication of these men and women.

I wandered through the cemetery. Tributes to individuals written on rather fine tombstones. Then I got to the church and went in and sat. It was a good-sized church —two towers. On the altar were a pair of candelabra made of wood from coffee trees. They were very pretty. A monk came in. I admired the candlesticks and he said, Please take them. I said thank you and I put money in the box while he was cleaning them up. Then he came out and said that he would bring them to the train for me. Off I went again, back toward town. I met John, also wandering. We got a bottle of wine and went to sit on a sort of high spot of land overlooking the jungle and the curving river as it wound itself south. And as the sun went down we heard the drums begin. Then the answering drums from another direction, then another and another. A symphony of drums. It was thrilling.

John talked. I don't even remember what he talked about but it was magic. Wasn't I lucky to be here. Adventure.

Got to the train. The candelabra got to the train. Betty was disgusted with me. I felt as if I'd played hooky—and secretly I was very pleased about it. Live dangerously. There's a lot to be said for sinning.

After a night in Stanleyville we flew to Entebbe. We were staying in a sort of country-club hotel, all very English in style. With golf and tennis and cricket. Well run. It was a great relief to the crew, who in our camp had been living in rather primitive conditions. Mine had been primitive too, but luxury primitive. They decided that they needed a pause of a few days before they moved on to quarters on a Lake Albert houseboat, the *Lugard II*, which was to take us up to the foot of Murchison Falls. The houseboat was docked at Butiaba, where we were to drive to the little chapel and village in the jungle which had been built for us. Robert Morley's chapel. The interior of his house was to be built in London on a stage, as Robert himself was there.

Entebbe was close to Kampala, which was quite a town. John had said he would take a taxi and drive to Kampala with me, but he got sidetracked so I went alone. At night. John is one of those men who, when they're not with you, forget you. I found a very nice black driver. He drove me around with pride in his country and pleasure that I was interested in seeing it. We drove to the palace, where Amin later lived; I sat on the hood of the taxi so that I could stand occasionally and look over the high wall. I walked into the local hospital, which seemed to me very spacious and pleasant. No one paid any attention to me, so I just wandered about. Very neat and attractive. This was 1951. The general situation for the blacks in Uganda was superior by far to their situation in the Congo, as far as a visitor could see in a casual walk about.

Next day the company had definitely made up its collective mind to stay in this comfortable hotel for several days. John decided that he would go on to the location and do a bit of hunting—elephants—until the company turned up. I thought to myself, Well! The probability is that I will never be here again. And rather than loll about the hotel, I think that I would like to go with John. Spiegel nearly had a fit. And quite right he was.

"Katie—setting off with John in a little plane—how can you—*how?* You may be killed. Then what . . . ?"

"Well, John may be killed."

"The hell with John. I can't control John, you know that. But you—I'm photographing you. You're a reasonable, decent human being."

"Yes, Sam—I have been—and I don't think it pays. I want adventure—I want to hunt elephants with John. Not to kill, just to see."

"Oh my God, Katie. Talk to Bogie. . . ."

Bogie came.

"Katie, what's happened to you? You're a decent human being."

"Not anymore I'm not. If you obey all the rules you miss all the fun. John has fun."

"John," says Bogie. "That son of a bitch has gotten to you."

"He's seeing Africa."

"You're making a picture."

"Yes, I'm making a picture, but I'm seeing life at the same time."

"She's gone," he said to Sam. "Under the spell."

"Listen, Katie—have you ever shot a gun?"

"Yes, Bogie—I'm a pretty good shot."

"Well, your friend John is not William Tell—in fact, when you get to that god-damned boat, you'd better throw a few cans over the side and see how good or how bad he is—and if the elephant charges . . . take my advice and run." He went off.

That night I worked on John's clothes. His pants—fly-buttoned—had no buttons. I got some buttons and sewed them on. They had just rotted off in the damp. Next morning we left.

We flew low over the jungle, scaring up the animals. It was extraordinary.

We arrived at the *Lugard II*, the house-boat, which was tied up to a dock. The skipper was a Scot, Captain Phimister. He had a house nearby, a charming house with wonderful skulls, especially the skull of a water buffalo. He said that he had given up hunting. When he had first got there he was very eager. Not anymore. True of most.

This indirect advice had no effect on us. We were eager! I was certainly not eager to kill anything, especially an elephant—perish the thought. But I was wild to know, what was it like? What do they do? The country—the animals.

We stowed away our junk.

The boat was quite good-sized. Each had a cabin on the deck with a bunk on one side, a chest of drawers and a chair on the other. With changing space between. And at the end a washbasin with a mirror over it. Very nicely arranged. The cabin door, louvered and clearing the floor and the ceiling by six inches. The johns and showers were aft on the same deck. John (and later Bogie) were to be on one side of the boat, I was on the other. The deck was broad enough so that I could put a deck chair outside my cabin door when I ate breakfast. Splendid.

We threw a few cans overboard and tried a few shots. Bogie was right. He—John—had beautiful guns and a passion for *le sport*. Not a great eye. But I was with him all the way. Adventure.

We started out the first morning about four. We had a white scout who carried a gun and a black scout who was not allowed to carry a gun. He carried a spear. We had a third cameraman—young, tall, English—Little John and Big John (Huston) and me. And we had two bearers. Each bearer would carry one object, be it a gun, a bag, a trunk, a matchbox. But he would carry only one object. I carried two leather bags on shoulder straps. One had a bottle of water. One had a few bananas and the inevitable box of English biscuits. I hate to be hungry.

Off we went in an old borrowed rattle-bang. We went about four miles and came to a sudden stop. Out of gas. What to do? No one had anything to write with or to write on. We scratched a message on a stone, left it on the front seat—"Help. No gas. John—Kate"—and walked on. By the time we got to where we should be it was too late—the elephants had gone to lie down in a safe spot near the high grass on the borders of the lake. Couldn't go there. Go home. Try again tomorrow. Lucky for us someone had come by our car, I think to find out whether we were still alive. And, seeing the car in such a peculiar place, had surmised our difficulty and got us some gas.

Next day—out earlier. Went to the spot. Started on a trail. We had a very thin linen handkerchief containing a handful of fine wood ashes. This was held by one of the boys. We were going through high grass. It was easy to tell that this was a trail used by elephants, as the grass was bent down in the direction we were going. And there were occasional droppings. Easy to tell also how recently the elephants had passed, by the freshness of the droppings. The wood ashes fell as a sort of smoke if you shook the handkerchief packet, and the direction of the smoke indicated the direction of the wind. The wind this day was only a tiny drift. On a slight rise of land downwind of us there was a sort of scrub forest of ratty-looking trees. We were walking along single file, each one carrying his own things. We were led by the black who knew this country. He carried a sort of spear about six or seven feet long. He was naked except for a pair of very short shorts. And he wore a dark-green Robin Hood hat pointed in crown and in brim. We all followed along.

All of a sudden there was the most terrifying sound-noise-yell-screech that I have ever heard. It just seized you by the seat of the pants and it raised you up and it shook you.

"What? What?"

"Elephant!" said John. "Trumpeting!" The scout pointed toward the rise of ground. We couldn't see them because of the dark and the high grass and trees. They were downwind of us and had got our scent.

John explained that we must make a big circle around in the direction we were already going and circle back to get downwind of them. The sun was already beginning to light the world. On we went.

We came to a different sort of terrain, where the grass was short and a few rocks—more open land. All of a sudden everyone stopped. A wild boar—female—followed by her several young pigs was calmly crossing our path.

Oh, what a shot, I thought. I started my movie camera—cartridge-loading—small—and started to walk very slowly and evenly toward the huge old boar. I wanted to get a close-up of her head. Slowly, slowly, bent over, I was walking. Oh, it was a great shot. The boar had stopped and was turning and looking right at me. Get that, I thought to myself. And began to go toward her. To get a big close-up of her head. Somehow from—it seemed from very far away—I heard a voice saying oh so quietly:

"Kate . . . Kate. Come back, Kate. . . ."

I stopped. What? Quiet! "Come back, Kate—slowly—"

Slowly I backed up. The boar turned away and continued down the trail with her young. Calmly John explained that the female wild boar with young is a very dangerous animal.

I said, "But, John, I didn't have a gun—I had a camera."

"Yes, dear," he said. "The pure in heart."

Later John gave me a tiny flat bronze of an African wild boar. "Portrait of your friend."

We continued our circling. The day was with us. And the heat. We were a bit north of the Equator here in Uganda, but it still hovered around eighty-five, ninety degrees all the time. Eighty at night. In the direct sun, of course, hotter. We came into a clearing and there before us, on top of a sort of rise but in the open—backed by scrub jungle—were about fifteen elephants. Varying sizes. Some seemed apprehensive, on the lookout—putting their trunks up in the air and sniffing this direction and that. They couldn't actually sniff us now, because we were downwind of them. They were wandering about. A family on an outing. It was a sort of high field—lots of rocks. We were too far away for a good shot. They are so big that—well, I myself could not begin to want to shoot anything unless I was hungry, but I know that it must be a very exciting sport. To me just to chase them and outwit them and find them and get close is what is exciting. Somehow a gun is an unfair advantage.

Well, honey, you've got a man here with an unfair advantage, and he's going to use it if he can.

The group had begun crawling slowly up the hill. John—Little John—the black scout —the white scout—two boys carrying this and that—and me.

The herd now began definitely to sense something and, like a wave or a wind drifting, all of a sudden they simply moved as one body into the scrub wood in back of them. Those huge creatures sort of evaporated.

So much for the kill.

We could hear them crashing about—then silence.

"We'll go in after them," said John.

Oh my God, I thought. We're not going to be dumb enough to do that.

"No," said the white scout.

"You're just yellow," said John with his usual tact. "We'll go in. . . ."

"Not with me," said the white scout.

He was a scrawny boy about twenty-two or twenty-three with a rather unattractive manner. Had no sense of how to handle John, who by then was hot, tired and frustrated and would have gone into the woods with no gun and tackled the elephant, the biggest elephant, single-handed.

"John, don't go into that wood. You haven't a chance—"

"What's that, dear? Oh—well, why don't you stay out here and wait for us . . . with *him*," he added (pointing at the boy who had opposed him).

Well, I thought, I'm going to have to follow that lunatic. . . .

Into the scrub forest we went. Caution at a low ebb. We got in about two hundred yards when there was a terrible roar and past us, missing us by about twenty-five feet, crashed the whole herd. Knocking down trees as they flew. And they were gone.

John stood transfixed. "Look at that . . . look at that! Isn't that great! What power! Magnificent! Well!"

Well, I thought, we're still here and he's absolutely crazy. And we're just lucky.

We started back for the car. On the way we shot a kudu—a sort of antelope. As we were really desperate for a good piece of meat, I didn't mind this. We tied his legs together and carried him on a small tree. There was a terrible scene where each one of us tried to cut its throat to bleed it. I can't remember whether the knife or the will to do it was too dull. But we were not too far from the car and we certainly didn't succeed in cutting its throat.

That was the end of the adventure.

And back at the houseboat we ate the kudu. It was a great treat. And *I* had been "hunting in Africa."

The crew had assembled. Bogie and Betty were there. Captain Phimister was set to go. We were in Lake Albert, moored to a dock close to a forest of very tall hardwood trees.

We went to take a look at the set for Morley's church.

"No good," said John.

"No good?"

"I have to start my picture with this shot. I'm on the sky—I'm on the treetops—then the tree trunks—then the cross—then the steeple, then the church. There's no steeple."

"He's a Methodist."

"Methodists don't have steeples, Mr. Huston."

"This one is going to."

"Methodists don't have crosses, John."

"These are going to." He took out a piece of paper. "Like this." And he drew it. "Don't you see, kid? No one really focuses on the fact that they are Methodists who

The end of the hunt—and finally a good dinner. Poor beastie.

don't use crosses and steeples. We have to establish that at once, the orthodox atmosphere. And what a charming church you've built. Yes, you've done a great job. And the perfect spot. I'm so pleased." And off they went to do his bidding, not knowing whether they were mad or glad. "Now let's go inside. — Ah, there it is, Katie. That's what you're going to have to play."

I looked at the organ. Went over and played "Work, for the Night Is Coming." That was the only hymn I knew.

"That's not what you play."

"I know."

"We have a record. I'll play it to you—come with me."

He played the record. He played it again. Then he took it off the table and dropped it. It smashed.

"Have you got another?"

"No."

"Give me a pencil." I quickly wrote it down in the key of C. I think it's key of C. I know less about music than an eight-year-old moron, but I have a good memory for a tune. I'll play it with the chords I know for "Work, for the Night Is Coming." It's all I could have done anyway. I can't play the piano.

They had started on the steeple. We went back to the boat.

It took them two days to rebuild the church. Poor Sam. In the meantime we rehearsed the scene without the church-full of natives who would be singing to Rosie's playing the organ to Robert Morley's double conducting the service. Lazy days. I played the hymn song well enough to suit John. I sang too.

It was a beautiful walk from the houseboat through the woods to the chapel—a good road past a very fancy lumber camp—past a few houses. I walked to and fro these semi-waiting days.

My father was very interested in different types of wood and I thought, Well, I'll go into the office of the lumber yard and get some samples. They were very polite, said they would get together a group and stick the names of the trees on little block samples. And would I like to see a tree felled? Would the company enjoy it?

Oh yes, but tomorrow we work. But the light is gone by four in the afternoon and then . . .

"Fine," he said, "four, about—in the afternoon. We'll be waiting."

That next morning I got made up and

drove to the chapel. I felt a bit odd. Sort of really weird. Well, don't mention it, because they can't work without you. It will pass.

I got my clothes on, went into the church. It was packed full of natives. And already it was hot as hell. And the air was thick with unwash. Oh dear.

I sat down on my stool and started to play the hymn. They started to sing. Their scale was certainly not our scale. Oh no. It was like nothing anyone had ever heard. All discords. A sound unlike anything I had ever even imagined. Oh dear.

And, creeping into the atmosphere, a smell unlike anything I had ever imagined. And my smellers are usually not very sensitive. But—oh dear!

Then a crawling illness began to overwhelm me. Good grief, I thought. I'm going to be sick. Where's the . . . Vi!

"I'll be right back."

I rushed for the ladies' outhouse. Opened the door. Went in—closed the door, or was about to . . .

Oh—my God, no!!! "Vi! — Someone!"

A black mamba! A snake.

A dangerous snake—a very dangerous snake!

I backed out of the hut, rushed for the trees, threw up.

"Get me a glass of water, Vi. . . ."

I went back into the church.

"There's a snake in the ladies' john—a black mamba," I yelled.

"Yes, we'll see to it. . . . A black mamba!" One of the crew rushed off.

I started to play the organ again.

It was a very trying day. I've got to keep going—I've got to last—I've got to see that tree felled. . . . I've got to lie down. Oh-h-h-h-h, I'm so sick. Go home, dear—go home—one more shot and . . . go.

"John—you've got to promise me that you will see that tree felled. And take Betty and Bogie and Vi and George and—promise!"

"Yes, honey. Yes, I promise."

"Don't you let me down—"

"No, honey—go now—trust me. . . ."

Trust him—well, no choice. I went back to the boat. Went to bed. Kept drinking a lot of water. Oh dear. Oh dear. I must have fallen asleep. . . .

Singing. What's that singing?

The door of my cabin opened—the whole group—and feeling no pain. And it was midnight.

They had all dutifully gone to the lumber camp at four for the "felling." Dear Katie—poor old Katie.

It had got very black. Storm-black. A wind was growing. They were driven to the tree by jeep. The huge tree was already cut half through. Suddenly—pouring rain—a violent gust of wind. A bolt of lightning. And the tree, instead of falling in the expected direction, was crashing toward them. Crashing! They scattered in every direction. Terrifying incident. Luckily no one was hurt.

They were all soaked to the skin. The head of the lumber camp took them home to his house. They drank his liquor. Put on all his spare clothes—caroused with him—and finally came back to the houseboat to serenade me. But I was past serenading and they finally went to bed. And funny old John. What did he do? He came back to my cabin.

"Just stay asleep, Katie dear. Stay asleep. Asleep—asleep . . ." And he rubbed my back with his smooth, strong hands. And my head and my neck and my hands and my feet. Such a blessing. Took the trouble from me. It is true—the laying on of hands. So quiet—so sweet—soothing. He was gentle.

Oh, John. Isn't he sweet!

Wonder what Bogie's thinking?

I slept. I don't remember when he stopped. Dear friend.

We started on (having finished the church sequence). Captain Phimister was an expert. It was fascinating to watch him skipper that bulky houseboat—she was a side-wheeler. We got to the end of Lake Albert, and seemingly there was nothing ahead but a huge field— swamp—high reeds. Phimister would back us up, then ram into the reeds at full tilt. After a few rams we pushed forward into open water. A stream this time, call it a river. High reed edges turning into jungle. Slowly rising away from the marshland. Oh, it was pretty. And it was so damned fascinating. We were in park land by this time. So no guns.

The game wardens collected the guns. Wise men, experienced. What people don't have, they can't use. That's right—they summed us up correctly.

Saw all manner of animals. The water was full of hippos. A herd of elephants stirred up by our noise fled right across the water —swam across, including a baby elephant. Adorable. Huge. We tried to get a shot (photograph)—too late. Birds, monkeys, flowers. Paradise. It was around these parts

that Hemingway had that bad forced landing—later. Remember . . .

We tied up at our final destination, a
sort of makeshift pier. We were at the foot
—well, far enough from the foot of the
Murchison Falls so that the dialogue was
safe. You couldn't actually see the Falls. But
if you went ashore and walked through a
carpet of crocodiles and hit the path up the
hill, you could get there. If you can picture.
We were in a sort of side cul de sac, a sort
of lake—small pond. At the sides it didn't
rise too steeply. There was a rather wide
open-water area and on the side away from
where we had the boat it was a sort of pas-
ture. We had the *Queen* and we had a big
raft for cameras and our two lights and sound.
The edges of the water were (I say again)
carpeted with crocodiles. And a crocodile is
an animal simply without charm. To see one
slither off the bank and under the water
giving you a baleful look just before he dis-
appears—"I'll get that leg," he's saying. "It's
just a question of time." And you won't
believe this. Often he just lies there on the
bank with his mouth wide open. Wide. And
birds pick his teeth. There's a tickbird too—
white—who picks the ticks off the elephants'
backs. The give and take of the jungle.

Shudders!

I must tell you about our life on board. We had a dining saloon amidships with several big tables. There was a room forward where people could sit and drink. The kitchen was below. They kept a few animals there too, I believe. Sometimes I'd hear a terrible scream or roar. Our dinner, I thought. Don't investigate.

As you know, I am a very early riser and Tahili Bokumba would bring me a tray and I sat out in my deck chair in pajamas and toweling robe and ate my breakfast. I could see great numbers of hippos in the water below. Their eyes huge. Just above water level. I'm sure that I wouldn't care to be swimming amongst them, but they look sort of dear and friendly. Teddy-bear style.

The weather—it was hot but not unbearable. It was damp; nothing dried. The sky was bright blue. The clouds were fat and full and cottony and it could change from bright sun to black rain in a flash and be pouring.

Save the camera. The camera. The umbrella here—cover the camera. Give me that blanket. Save the sound. Cover the mike.

They didn't pay much attention to the people—they'd dry off. As usual, my hair was my greatest problem. Save the curls.

140

Wet or dry, Bogie and I looked more or less the same. The rain would literally pour down—pour. The cloud would simply open. A deluge. And then it would disappear. Out came the sun. And we'd start work again. We had the *Queen* and another boat with a motor to lug us back and forth from the *Lugard II*. Also to take us to shore to change costume or to go to the john. We'd have lunch back on the big boat.

The food problem was interesting—hard to get meat and eggs, but easier to prepare than at our camp in the Congo. Very good, considering. The dining saloon was long skinny tables—chairs either side. At night the lights had to be on and the lights were hanging over the tables. Anyone coming in had to open the door, which gave onto the deck. Whereupon clouds of curious moth-like creatures would swarm in and rush for the lights—and they would be immediately electrocuted. And drop—often into one's dinner. Dead or alive, sort of sticky. You'd have to pick them out of your dish and they were hard to find if they fell into your mashed potatoes or the creamed sauce. Bogie was a light eater. And this situation did not increase his appetite. John was not a big eater either. They came to the table well fortified.

Bogie was funny. A generous actor. And a no-bunk person. He just did it. He was an actor who enjoyed acting. Knew he was good. Always knew his lines. Always was on time. Hated anything false. Hated his hairpiece as he began to need one. Liked to play with a hat or cap on—something—anything on. That damned hairpiece. At the beginning of a day when he was wearing it he was grumpy —impatient. Then he'd forget about it and was fine. At the end of the day he was tired. So until he'd had a drink or two he was grumpy. He'd come to the table and sort of begin to needle me. I was adorable and malleable and well trained to handle the male grumps. I just agreed with everything he said. Then he'd smooth out. He was an extraordinarily decent fellow. Fair—forthright—uncomplicated. Fun too—a good sense of humor. Devilish if he thought you were a phony. Like a cat with a mouse, he'd never let you off. He and John drank their share. I was almost a teetotaler. And really thought they were pathetic to have to rely on liquor as a stimulant. Poor weak things, I thought.

Everyone went to bed early on the boat

—at least I think they did. As I say this I realize that I never stayed up to find out what they did, because I was always the earliest in and the earliest out.

The days came and went. No real incidents. I went up the hill with the purser, one day that I was free. He was a wood carver and I told him that I would like to get a piece of ebony to make a cane for my father. We found a tree about the right size —three inches through. It is very rough bark and hard as nails. He cut a piece the appropriate length. And I still have the cane and a six-inch sample of the original tree. Beautiful.

After we'd been on the boat about a week or ten days, people in the company began to get sick. Sick to their stomachs. I had had the one attack when we did the scene in the chapel; then I had pretty much recovered. Now I began to get sick again. I would eat and throw up, but I had to keep going because without me there was no work. I would do the best I could. But eating was very hazardous, especially anything hot. Being a urologist's daughter, I decided to flood myself with water. The great cure. In this case, it didn't seem to work. Gradually others began ailing. The sound crew was deci-

Bogie Alnutt.

Rosie Hepburn

mated. The head sound man had to lie down, otherwise he would fall down, so he worked from the horizontal. Jack Cardiff, the brilliant first cameraman, was laid low with malaria—a recurrence for him—and also the blight which seemed to be attacking so many of us. We were crawling. I lost twenty pounds and I was thin to begin with. It was weird. The doctor on the boat was totally confused. He had analyzed the water tank—it was O.K. Finally he put everyone on bottled water. Still disaster. Finally we lost so many of the crew that they said to me, "For God's sake, lie down. We're insured if you're sick." So I lay down and began to take one of the cure-all drugs. Tahili Bokumba slept at my door. He helped me to the john, then sat at the john door waiting, which was most embarrassing. I noticed that he too had begun to look a bit odd. On questioning, I found out that he and the boy who had come from the Congo with John Huston were suffering because in the Congo they had a basic diet of rice and here they had maize, which they did not like. I quickly got hold of my friend the purser and he said they had rice and I said, Give it all to me. We English don't give a damn—we're potato people. So he gave me all the rice he had. And I kept it in my bottom bureau drawer and would dole it out by the cupful to my two black friends. I was trying to make it last.

After taking the cure drug for two days, I said that I would die if I went on. My spirit was gone. I ached in every joint—couldn't keep food down. The cure was worse than the blight; I must just crawl along without the antibiotic. Because—with it—I really could not function at all.

So back to work. To try to finish what little we had left to do.

Now, all this time neither Bogie nor John had been sick at all. They were fine.

Then the doctor decided to test the bottled water. Yes—you're right. The bottled water was polluted. And I—the queen of water drinking—the urologist's prize—was the sickest. And those two undisciplined weaklings had so lined their insides with alcohol that no bug could live in the atmosphere. Well, Katie, what do you say to that? There wasn't much I could say. I took to champagne. Well, it really was a very good joke on me. Especially as privately I had felt so completely superior to that unhealthy pair.

OVERLEAF AND FOLLOWING PAGES: Angling in on the *Queen*.

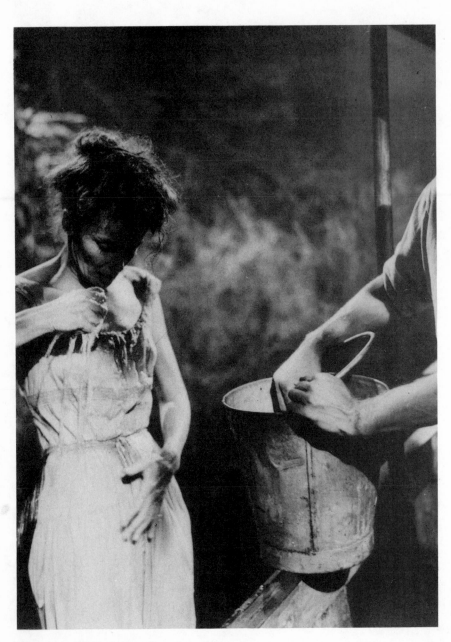

Dampening down for the next shot.

We had practically finished everything at this point and were about to head back to Entebbe. John wanted to get shots of Bogie and me in the miles of high reeds before we come out into the lake. And at the point when we discover the German ship. And at the point where Bogie is lying on the floor so sick and Rosie thinks that he is going to die and she climbs the mast to look for help. Sam Spiegel felt that we should get out while the getting was good, before everyone really collapsed. John persisted—no, we needed those shots. He was immovable, as usual. Sam gave him a limited time. Then he pulled the crew. Left Bogie and me and Bogie's hairpiece and some makeup, but no makeup man. We had Ted Scaife to photograph us. No dialogue, so no sound. I put on my makeup and I put on Bogie's hairpiece for him. Did my own hair. And we got the shots which John wanted.

It is important to know that there was no way to shoot Bogie and me actually in the water. The water on the fringes of the lake—stream—whatever—was polluted with a bug called *bilharzia*. The bug comes from human excrement or urine and lingers in reeds, etc. It can enter the body through the body openings or through the pores. My father, being a doctor and worrying about this, had sent me to a man named Macdonald at the London Hospital for Tropical Diseases. I went to see him in his office before I set out for Africa. He hardly looked up from the paper he was working on. "Don't go into the water, Katharine. Don't go into the water anywhere. I could go in in certain places because I know which places are O.K. Don't you go in anywhere. You're too ignorant. If your feet—shoes—get wet from the bilge, take your shoes off. Your stockings off. Wash your feet in good water. Dry them carefully. Powder them. This *bilharzia* is a most unpleasant disease—used to be fatal. Is hard to cure. Sort of large boils in the urinary tract—kidneys, etc. Don't go into the water."

"I won't, sir."

I didn't.

No one did.

I think Edwina Booth, who in the silent days did a picture in Africa, died of this disease. Well—boils in the kidneys! Ouch. We were careful about that, I'll tell you.

So—back to Entebbe. Goodbye—goodbye—dear Tahili Bokumba. I gave him money for his service and presents for his friendship. A traveling clock. My Burberry raincoat. And to go with it, we bought him a regular straw hat that he wanted desperately—a status symbol. And off he went—working his way back to the Congo, his pockets full of money. And his spirit—well, it had been a wonderful adventure. For a month or so—a kind of freedom from the psychological imprisonment of being looked upon as inferior. He was a very decent person—honest as the day is long. And thoughtful and fun as my helper and dear when I was ill. I remember observing one thing which struck me very powerfully. I would look serious or worried or trying to be sympathetic—or solemn. And I would receive back an absolutely impenetrable expression. A wall. But if I smiled or laughed, he did too. The universal language. This amazed me. I would have thought that tears were the things which bound us together, but no— smiles, laughter—and they warmed up immediately. Understand my ridiculous self— thank you—yes. We are ridiculous, aren't we —black—white—yellow? If we couldn't have some laughter we would crumble. Color be damned. We must laugh together.

The last few days there, sick as I was, I was still moved by the beauty of the country—by its vigor. It had been such an extraordinary experience and it was ending.

We were going back to London. Would I ever come back here? Oh, I hope—I hope.

We flew from Entebbe. Stopped over to refuel—got off and into an oven. Walked out of the plane and nearly died of the dry desert heat—not like Uganda or the Congo. Then to Cairo, a five-hour layover. At that time Americans were not allowed to leave the airport. We tried to get permission but failed. I thought that they might let us take a peek at the pyramids, but no such luck. John and I had a paperback, *Miss Hargreaves*, which we were reading. We read the whole novel on the trip back. Good part for me. We bought it. We never made it.

Back in London. We had taken over a tiny studio. The first thing we shot was the scene with Robert Morley and Rosie (his sister). Then Morley gets sick and then he dies. It was a charming, rather large ground-floor tropical house. The minister's house.

But I'm jumping ahead. I was again staying at Claridge's. We—Constance Collier, Phyllis Wilbourn and I. I still had the residue of the African blight and I thought I'd better find out what could be done, as I still had a desire to lose my lunch whenever I ate hot food. Apparently the intestinal tract can get into bad habits and has to be coaxed back into more civilized ways. I had the name of an internist, Sir Horace Evans —I had got his name from my dad and also found out that he was very famous. The Queen's physician, later to become Lord Evans. I called his office and was informed that he would be delighted to come to see me. He came. In a morning suit. The vulgarity of having to bring up the subject of my intestines to this tall, slim and extremely formal Britisher—so gorgeous, really—embarrassed me almost to the point of silence. And the thought of his going off with specimens of this and that. Oh dear. But that is what happened. Later we became good friends. Anyway, he cured me.

Back to the studio:

There were several stages—one with Robert Morley's and Rosie's house—on the other they were constructing a tank for the underwater sequences and the sequences where we drag the *Queen* through the reeds. And the German boat was being constructed on a high platform. All the scenes where we had actually to be in the water.

The first scene was with Morley—the one I began to tell you about—where he started getting sick and beaten, and then when he died and Rosie was left alone—

scared—I didn't know what to do. John said to me, "Just do whatever comes into your head and we'll follow you and I'll keep turning. Tell me when you're ready. O.K. Boys, turn 'em when . . ." Well—glory be, I thought. What does he want . . . ? "O.K., John, I'm ready."

When you do a very serious scene it requires a sort of deep . . . well, not a sort of . . . it just requires super-deep concentration. So I was naturally excited and ticking away trying to do my bit: Poor dead brother. And what am I going to do? And I wandered and I stood and I wept and I stopped and I went on and on—grunting and groaning and trying and thinking, Won't he ever cut, and overacting and finally everyone screamed with laughter. A practical joke on dear old Katie. Is that a joke? To make me go on and on and *on?*

Well, do you think that's funny?

No, neither did I.

So—that's bloody stupid. I agree.

I was furious. That fool John.

Funny as a baby's open grave.

Well, save your breath—he's not going to change. Take the bad with the good.

That's my genius!

He'd been on the picture for some time.

Hello Morley. Want a lift?

Was boredom beginning to set in? Was it taking too long? Was he looking for new thrills?

Well, he didn't have to wait long.

The first tank scene was going to be done Monday. It was Saturday afternoon (we worked a six-day week in those days). We all went over to look at the tank on Saturday—late afternoon—after work. It was being filled. Ready for Bogie and me.

On John's bike . . . I've obviously lost my mind.

When we got there Monday we found that late on Sunday the tank had burst. The whole end of it had just burst. And with such force that the crane which was standing next to it was twisted as though it were a hairpin. The huge door of the stage was smashed down. It was really quite terrifying. Lucky that they had filled it a day early—I hate to think of what might have happened otherwise. We quickly got a tank at EMI which was not in use and did the underwater work there— of the broken propeller, etc., where you had to see Charlie and Rosie in deep water. Oh, how Bogie hated that swimming—he froze. I swim all winter in Long Island Sound: ten degrees above zero and with a north wind blowing is my record. One of my more irritating qualities. Why do I do it? I think to be irritating. Don't you? Why else?

The tank—about four feet deep with the reeds—was done back at our studio. I remember that before a scene it had to be cleared of old tea buns which had been thrown in absent-mindedly after the tea break.

Then watching the sinking of the German gunboat and the slightly silly and abrupt finish. We had definitely got to the "Well, that's done" stage. Hurry hurry . . .

The scene on the gunboat. Well, the boat was constructed on a high scaffolding, with only a sky view. Just in an open space on the lot. That was a very weak scene, but it satisfied. Charlie and Rosie won!

That's about it.

Oh—the leeches. I knew you were going to ask about those. They brought in some real leeches—poor Bogie. They are really repellent. A glass full of the slimy things. "What's the matter, Bogie—you scared of a leech? Try one," I said.

"You try it first, kid."

Well, ugh. I just couldn't. They *are* revolting. And he had to be covered with them. Ugh.

So the rest of that day was spent trying to find—invent—a material that would stick to Bogie's skinny frame. There he sat—and everyone would come in and see if his or her concoction would stick. He was funny, sitting there. What an odd man. So—how shall I put it—so pure. Like a little kid. Dear Bogie. I'll never forget that close-up of him after he kisses Rosie, then goes around in back of the tank and considers what has happened. His expression—the wonder of it all—life.

Well. No more to tell, except, as you

Trying to fit Bogie up with the leeches.

Back in London, in the tank.

perhaps remember, Bogie won the Academy Award for his performance as Charlie Alnutt.

We were back in California. Betty called and said that she was giving a big party after the Awards—for Bogie.

"But, Betty, he hasn't won it!"

"Well, he's going to win it. So are you."

"But, Betty . . . you just can't count your chickens . . ."

"What do you mean, Katie? You mean you think he's not going to . . . ?"

"Well, no. I think. I hope. But, golly Moses, Betty—a big party, and suppose . . ."

"I won't suppose anything. He's going to win it."

Well—he did.

And why not? He sank that German gunboat, didn't he? He got down the rapids—you didn't think he could do that, did you? Well, he did!

And that's really just about it. Of course, I mean for us it ended. We had done all that we could do—packed up our junk—come home. The picture was cut and released and seemed to please people, which is always a great relief. And it seems to go on pleasing people. And this kind of memory of its conception and its birth is fun for me.

It's strange being a movie actor. The product goes out—it's popular—it's unpopular—or it's somewhere in between. And it's always to me a real part of myself. I mean it represents my own decision to do it: Was I wise? Was I dumb? I've tried never to do anything just for the money. I do it because I love it—the idea and the characters. And, my oh my, it is great when you—when the people like it too and make it theirs—that is the real reward.

So, suddenly, thirty-five years have rushed by. Bogie has gone. Spiegel has gone. The *Queen* herself is still alive—so are John and Betty and Peter and I.

Now, what do you suppose ever happened to Charlie and Rosie? Where did they live? Did they stay in Africa? I always thought they must have. And lots of little Charlies and Rosies. And lived happily ever after. Because that's what we wanted them to do. And every summer they take a trip in the old *Queen*—and laugh and laugh and laugh and laugh. . . .

PHOTOGRAPHIC CREDITS

Front photo: Eliot Elisofon, LIFE magazine, © Time Inc.

i: Courtesy of Arthur E. Lemon, Romulus Films/Horizon Pictures, and the Estate of Sam Spiegel. © 1951, Horizon Management, Inc.; copyright renewed 1979.

ii: Eliot Elisofon, LIFE magazine, © Time Inc.

vii: Eliot Elisofon, LIFE magazine, © Time Inc.

x: Courtesy of the Ben Carbonetto Collection, Romulus Films/Horizon Pictures, and the Estate of Sam Spiegel. © 1951, Horizon Management, Inc.; copyright renewed 1979.

26: Courtesy of Lauren Bacall.

44: Eliot Elisofon, LIFE magazine, © Time Inc.

45: Courtesy of the Wisconsin Center for Film and Theater Research, Romulus Films/Horizon Pictures, and the Estate of Sam Spiegel. © 1951, Horizon Management, Inc.; copyright renewed 1979. Photographed by Arthur E. Lemon.

54: Eliot Elisofon, LIFE magazine, © Time Inc.

55: Eliot Elisofon, LIFE magazine, © Time Inc.

58-9: Eliot Elisofon, LIFE magazine, © Time Inc.

67: Courtesy of the Wisconsin Center for Film and Theater Research, Romulus Films/Horizon Pictures, and the Estate of Sam Spiegel. © 1951, Horizon Management, Inc.; copyright renewed 1979.

69: Eliot Elisofon, LIFE magazine, © Time Inc.

73: Eliot Elisofon, LIFE magazine, © Time Inc.

74: Eliot Elisofon, LIFE magazine, © Time Inc.

80: Courtesy of Arthur E. Lemon, Romulus Films/Horizon Pictures, and the Estate of Sam Spiegel. © 1951, Horizon Management, Inc.; copyright renewed 1979.

81: Courtesy of the Wisconsin Center for Film and Theater Research, Romulus Films/Horizon Pictures, and the Estate of Sam Spiegel. © 1951, Horizon Man-

Films/Horizon Pictures, and the Estate of Sam Spiegel. © 1951, Horizon Management, Inc.; copyright renewed 1979. Photographed by Arthur E. Lemon.

108: Courtesy of James Hendricks and the National Film Archive, London; Romulus Films/Horizon Pictures; and the Estate of Sam Spiegel. © 1951, Horizon Management, Inc.; copyright renewed 1979. Photographed by Arthur E. Lemon.

112-13: Courtesy of the Wisconsin Center for Film and Theater Research, the Academy of Motion Picture Arts and Sciences, Romulus Films/Horizon Pictures, and the Estate of Sam Spiegel. © 1951, Horizon Management, Inc.; copyright renewed 1979. Photographed by Arthur E. Lemon.

130: Courtesy of the Wisconsin Center for Film and Theater Research, the Academy of Motion Picture Arts and Sciences, Romulus Films/Horizon Pictures, and the Estate of Sam Spiegel. © 1951, Horizon Management, Inc.; copyright renewed 1979. Photographed by Arthur E. Lemon.

137: Courtesy of the Wisconsin Center for

Film and Theater Research.

144-45: Eliot Elisofon, LIFE magazine, © Time Inc.

148-49: Courtesy of Arthur E. Lemon, Romulus Films / Horizon Pictures, and the Estate of Sam Spiegel. © 1951, Horizon Management, Inc.; copyright renewed 1979.

150: Courtesy of Katharine Hepburn, Romulus Films / Horizon Pictures, and the Estate of Sam Spiegel. © 1951, Horizon Management, Inc.; copyright renewed 1979. Photographed by Arthur E. Lemon.

151: Courtesy of Arthur E. Lemon, Romulus Films/Horizon Pictures, and the Estate of Sam Spiegel. © 1951, Horizon Management, Inc.; copyright renewed 1979.

152-53, 160: Courtesy of the Wisconsin Center for Film and Theater Research, the Academy of Motion Picture Arts and Sciences, Romulus Films / Horizon Pictures, and the Estate of Sam Spiegel. © 1951, Horizon Management, Inc.; copyright renewed 1979. Photographed by Arthur E. Lemon.

161: Courtesy of the Ben Carbonetto Collection, Romulus Films / Horizon Pictures, and the Estate of Sam Spiegel. © 1951, Horizon Management, Inc.; copyright renewed 1979. Photographed by Arthur E. Lemon.

164: Courtesy of the Ben Carbonetto Collection, Romulus Films/Horizon Pictures, and the Estate of Sam Spiegel. © 1951, Horizon Management, Inc.; copyright renewed 1979. Photographed by Arthur E. Lemon.

165: Courtesy of the Wisconsin Center for Film and Theater Research, Romulus Films/Horizon Pictures, and the Estate of Sam Spiegel. © 1951, Horizon Management, Inc.; copyright renewed 1979. Photographed by Arthur E. Lemon.

176: Courtesy of Katharine Hepburn, Romulus Films/Horizon Pictures, and the Estate of Sam Spiegel. © 1951, Horizon Management, Inc.; copyright renewed 1979. Photographed by Arthur E. Lemon.

168-69: Courtesy of Arthur E. Lemon, Romulus Films/Horizon Pictures, and the Estate of Sam Spiegel. © 1951, Horizon Management, Inc.; copyright renewed 1979. Photographed by Arthur E. Lemon.

The publishers hope that this
Large Print Book has brought
you pleasurable reading.
Each title is designed to make
the text as easy to see as possible.
G.K. Hall Large Print Books
are available from your library and
your local bookstore. Or, you can
receive information by mail on
upcoming and current Large Print Books
and order directly from the publishers.
Just send your name and address to:

G.K. Hall & Co.
70 Lincoln Street
Boston, Mass. 02111

or call, toll-free:

1-800-343-2806

A note on the text
Large print edition designed by
Bernadette Montalvo.
Composed in 18 pt Plantin
on a Xyvision 300/Linotron 202N
by Marilyn Ann Richards
of G.K. Hall & Co.